By Karol Ann Krakauer

Picture Songs 1 A
for beginning pianists

Picture Songs Classical 1 B

Picture Songs 1C

Picture Songs 2
Scales - Chords - Fingering -Timing
& Other Music Theory
to be studied along with book 3 & above

Picture Songs 2B Chord Tricks

Picture Songs 3
Songs of God and Country

Picture Songs 4
More Songs of God and Country

Coming soon:
Picture Songs 5
Spanish Songs
with bilingual lyrics

Picture Songs 6
Songs from Around the World
with bilingual lyrics

PICTURE SONGS 1B
CLASSICAL

for beginning pianists

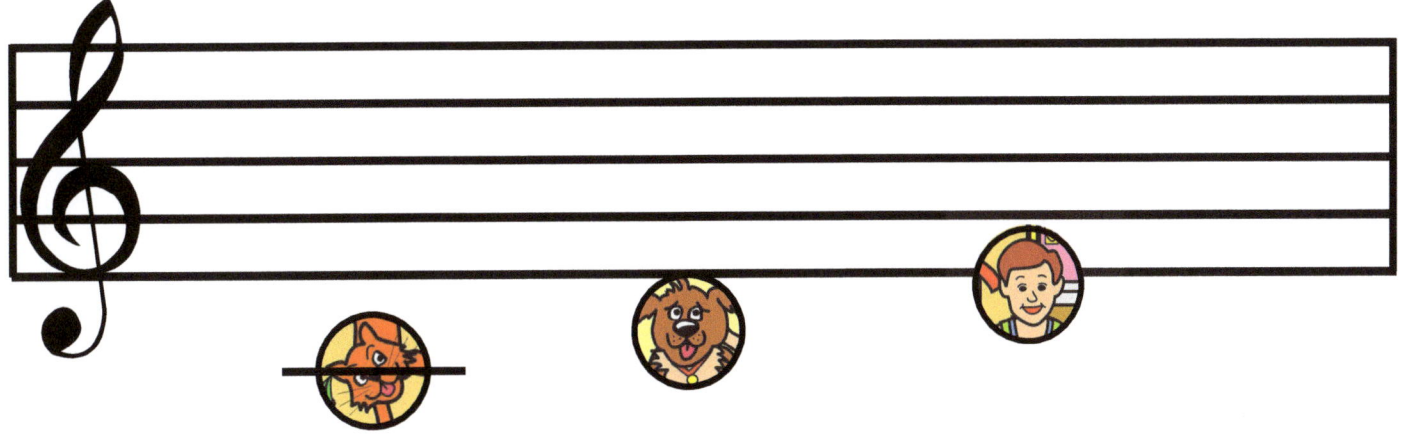

by Karol Ann Krakauer
Fort Collins, Colorado
2018

COPYRIGHT © 2018
by Karol Ann Krakauer
available at Amazon.com

Illustrations copyright 2004 by
Evans-Perucca

All rights reserved. No part of this book may be reproduced or transmitted in any form or by any means, electronic or mechanical, without the permission of the publisher.

picturesongs@outlook.com

To my mother who brought music to my life.

Table of Contents

INTRODUCTION	9
PIANO BLOCKS	10
MIDDLE C	11
BASS CLEF Use your left hand	12
TREBLE CLEF Use your right hand	13
CLIMGING THE LADDER	14
STEPS Left Hand	16
STEPS Right Hand	17
SKIPS Three Note Chords	18
STEPS AND SKIPS Two Note Chords	19
ODE TO JOY	20
GET READY FOR THE NEXT SONG	28
MOVING YOUR FINGERS	29
EINE KLEINE NACHTMUSIK	30
JESUS CHRIST IS RISEN TODAY	40
CLIMBING THE LADDER AGAIN	42
HALLELUJAH CHORUS	44
JESUS LOVES ME	50

INTRODUCTION

This book presents more songs in pictures. Play it as soon as you finish your first Picture Songs for beginning pianists book. It is designed to increase your repertoire (collection of songs) before you tackle Picture Songs 2, 3 and 4. In the beginning of this book you will want to review your steps and skips which you just learned in Picture Songs 1 for beginning pianists.

We will introduce you to which fingers you will use on notes and also how to count your rhythm.

The songs in this book are famous pieces. You might like to listen to them being played on your computer.

PIANO KEY BLOCKS

Sets of 7 blocks picturing the cat, dog, grandma, grandson Eddie, front door, back door and apple are available for placement on the piano keys. The blocks can be purchased by e-mailing picturesongs@outlook.com. If you have not already purchased your blocks now may be the time. You may want 2 or 3 sets to place in different neighborhoods on the key board to expand your playing.

MIDDLE C

Put your first cat C block in the very middle of the piano keyboard. This is "middle C". On music middle C can always be found between the two sets of lines. And middle C always has a little horizontal line through it.

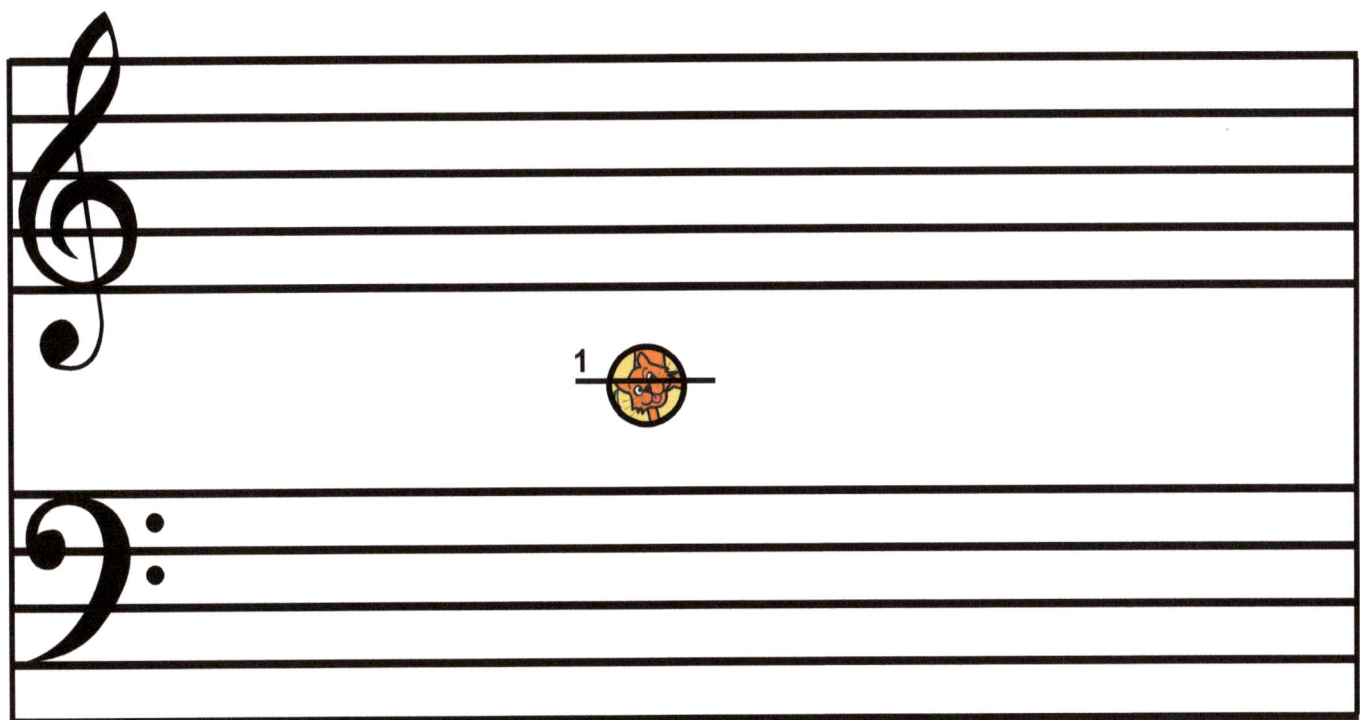

BASS CLEF
Use your left hand

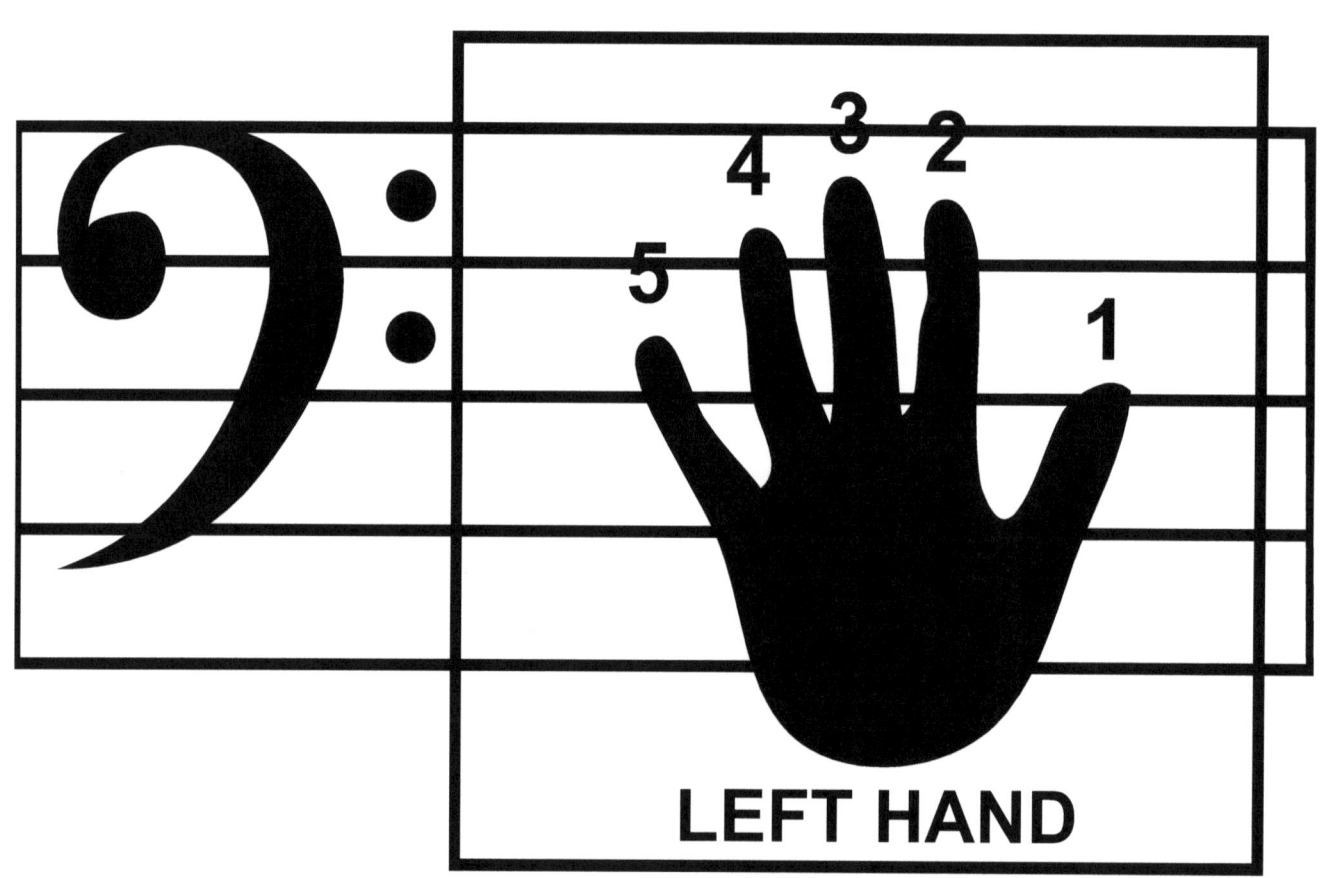

TREBLE CLEF
Use your right hand

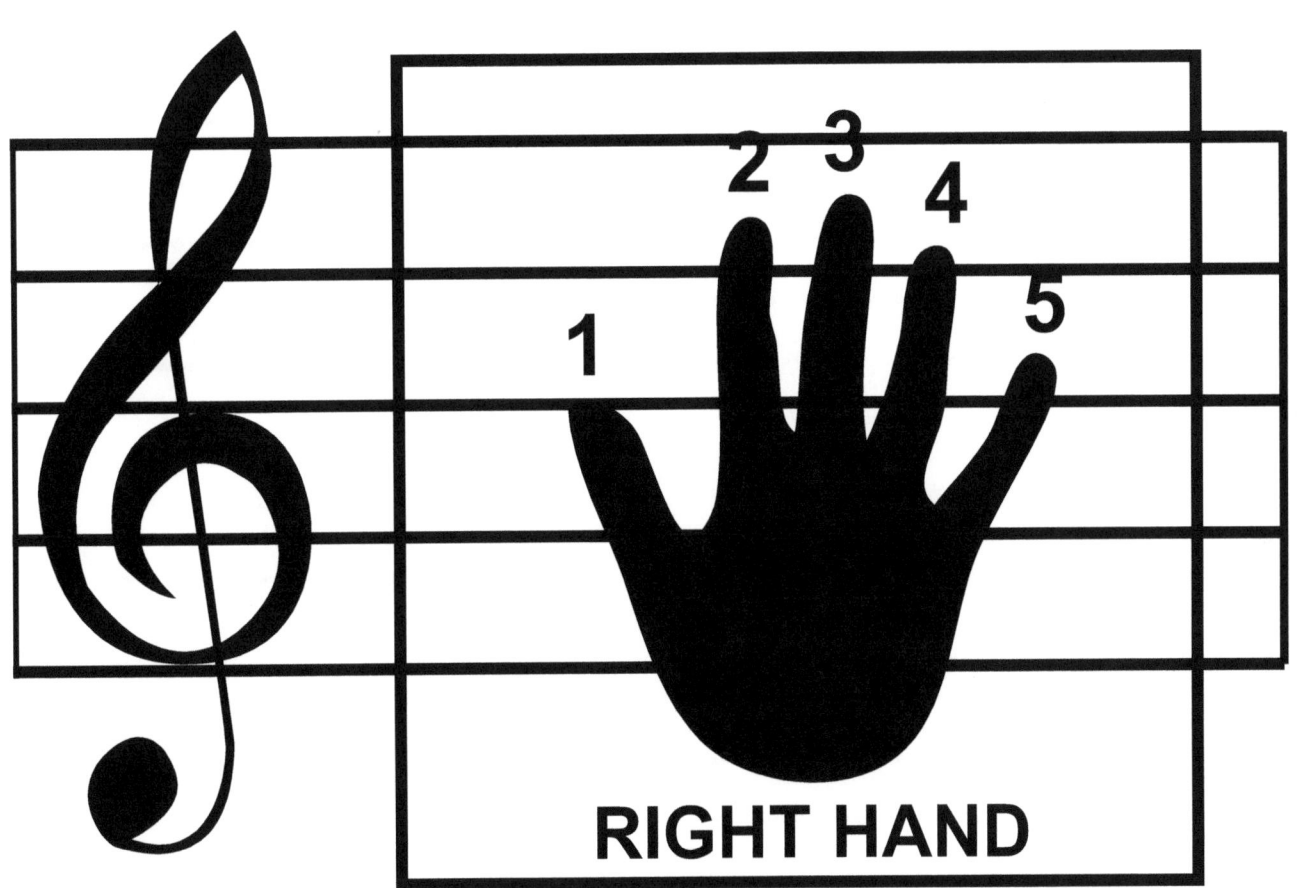

CLIMBING THE LADDER

These big lines are the ladder for climbing up and down the music pages. Climb up to the high notes and down to the low notes.

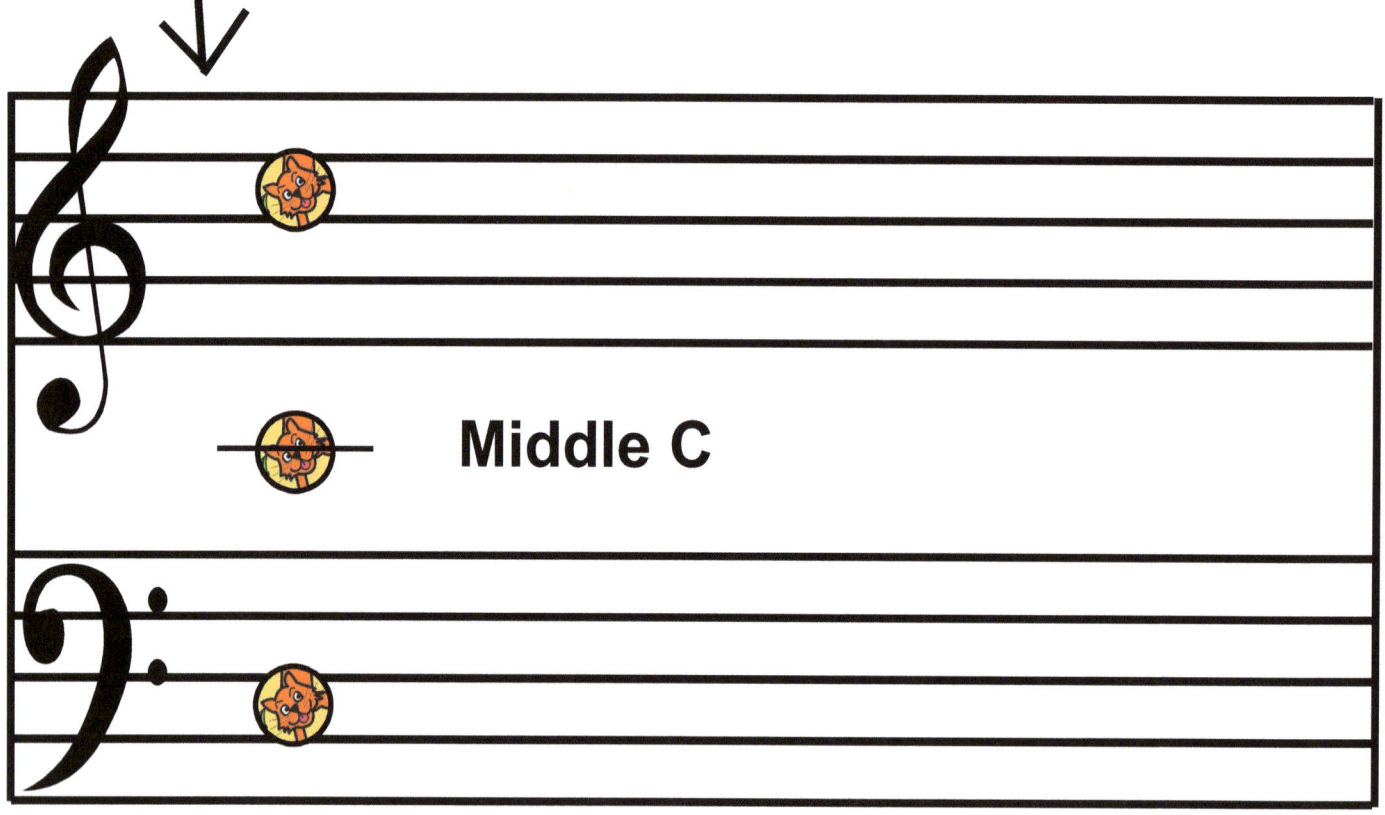

Middle C

Up the ladder to the high sounding notes on your music pages.

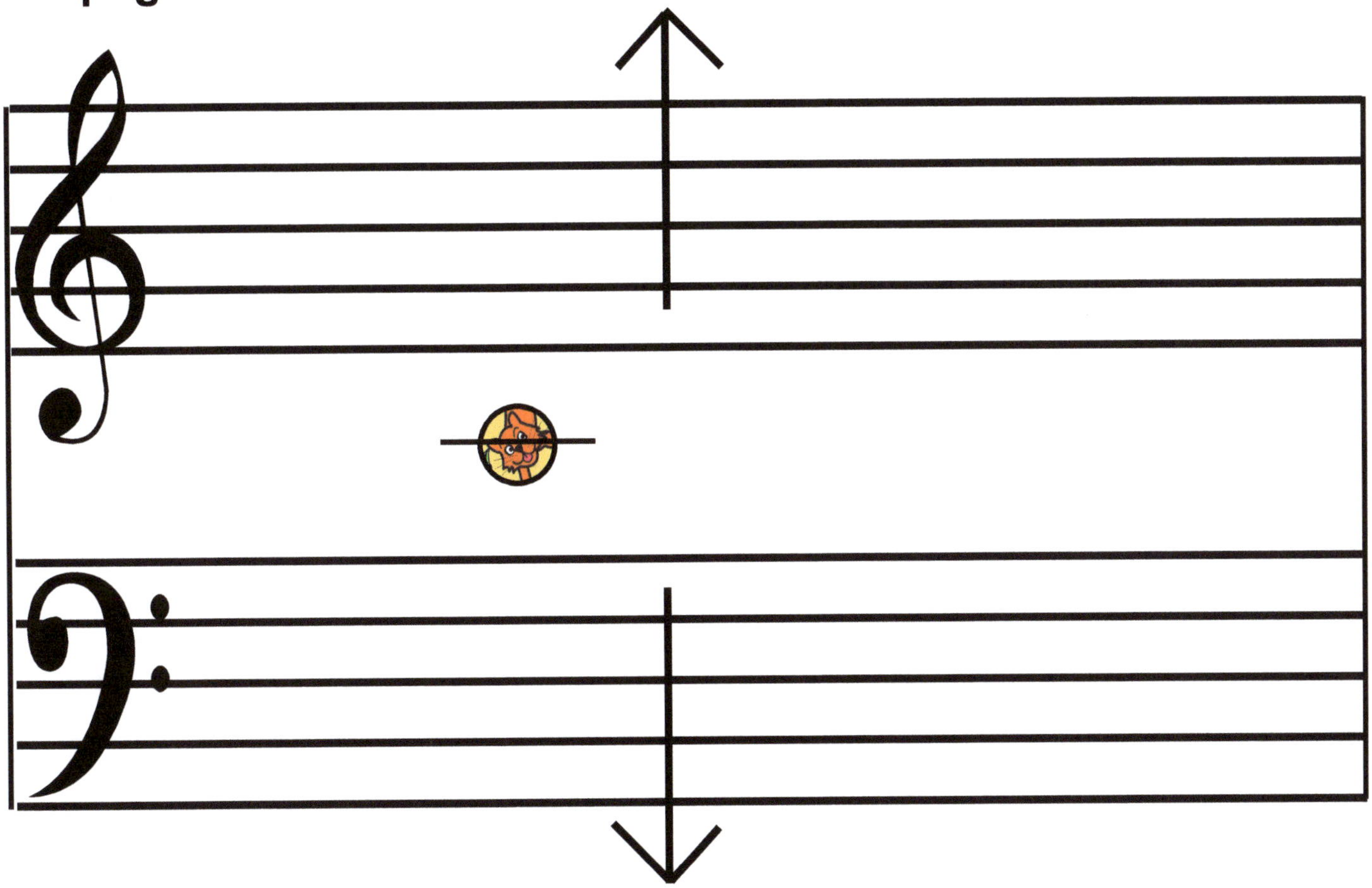

Down the ladder to the low sounding notes on your music pages.

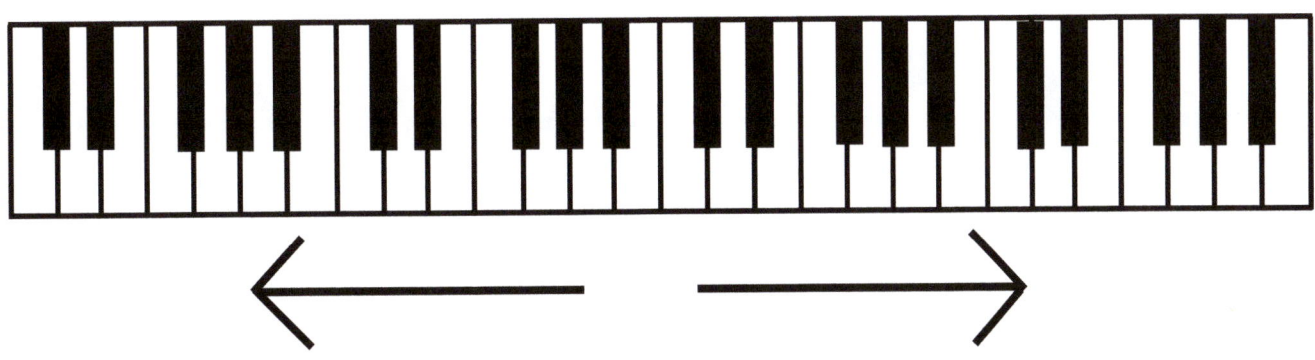

Down the piano to the low sounding notes.

Up the piano to the high sounding notes.

STEPS
Left Hand

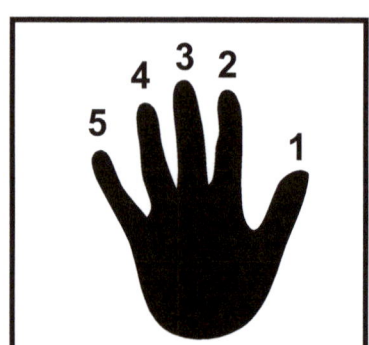

Play your steps pretending you are climbing up a ladder from Cat C to Grandma G with your left hand.

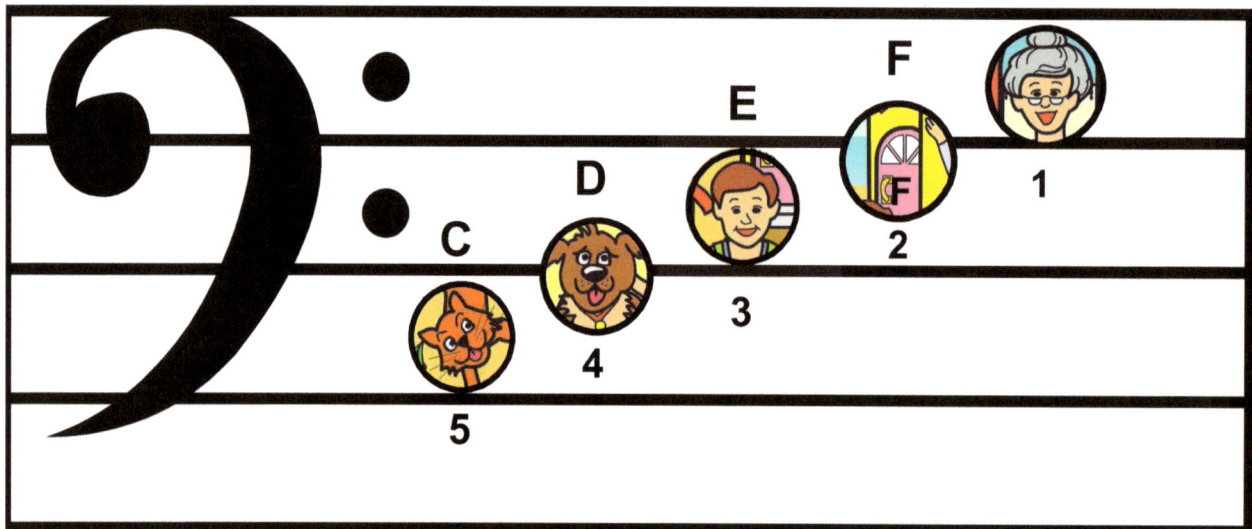

Now play your steps pretending your are climbing down a ladder from Grandma G to Cat C with your left hand.

STEPS
Right Hand

Now with your right hand pretend you are climbing up a ladder from Cat C to Grandma G.

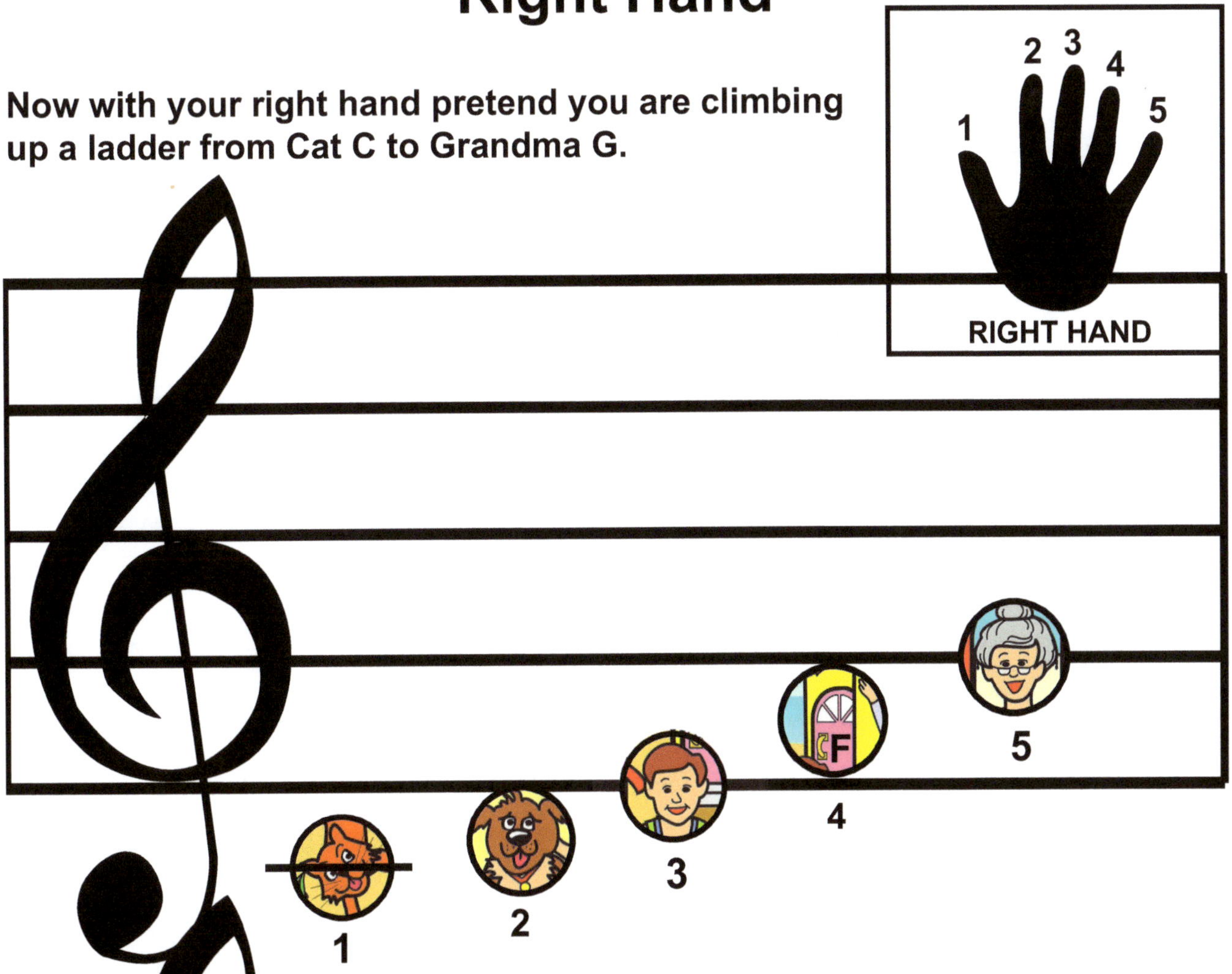

RIGHT HAND

Now play your steps pretending you are climbing down a ladder from Grandma G to Cat C with your right hand.

SKIPS

Three Note Chords
Left Hand

Three note chords are made out of skips. Once your hand is large enough, play the skips below (fingers 5-3-1) all together at the same time. When notes are stacked up like this you always play them all together.

C Chord - play all 3 notes together

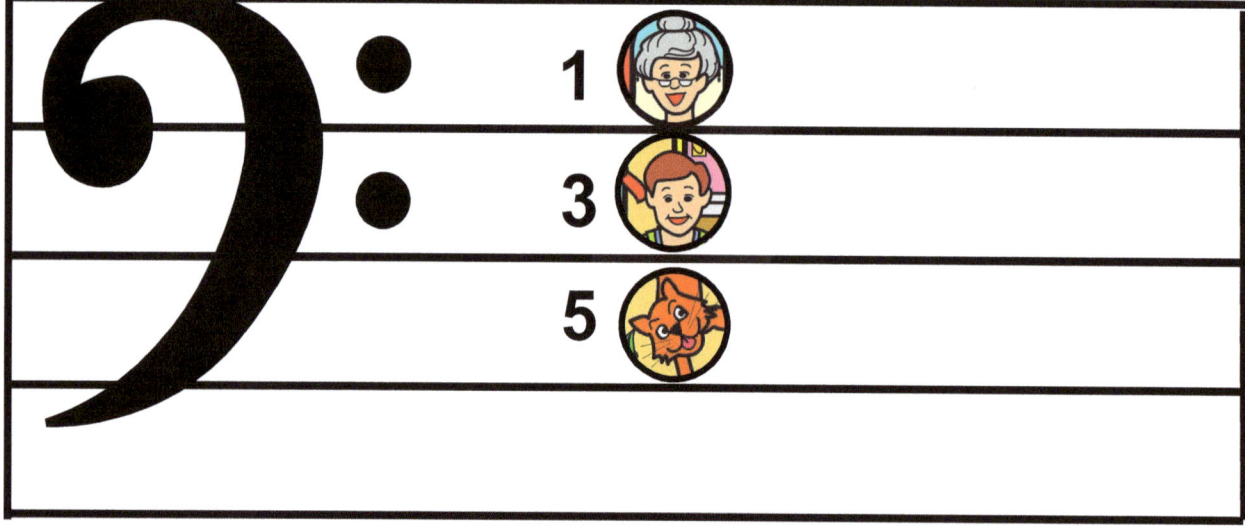

STEPS AND SKIPS
Two Note Chords
Left Hand

G7 Chord - play both notes together

F Chord - play both notes together

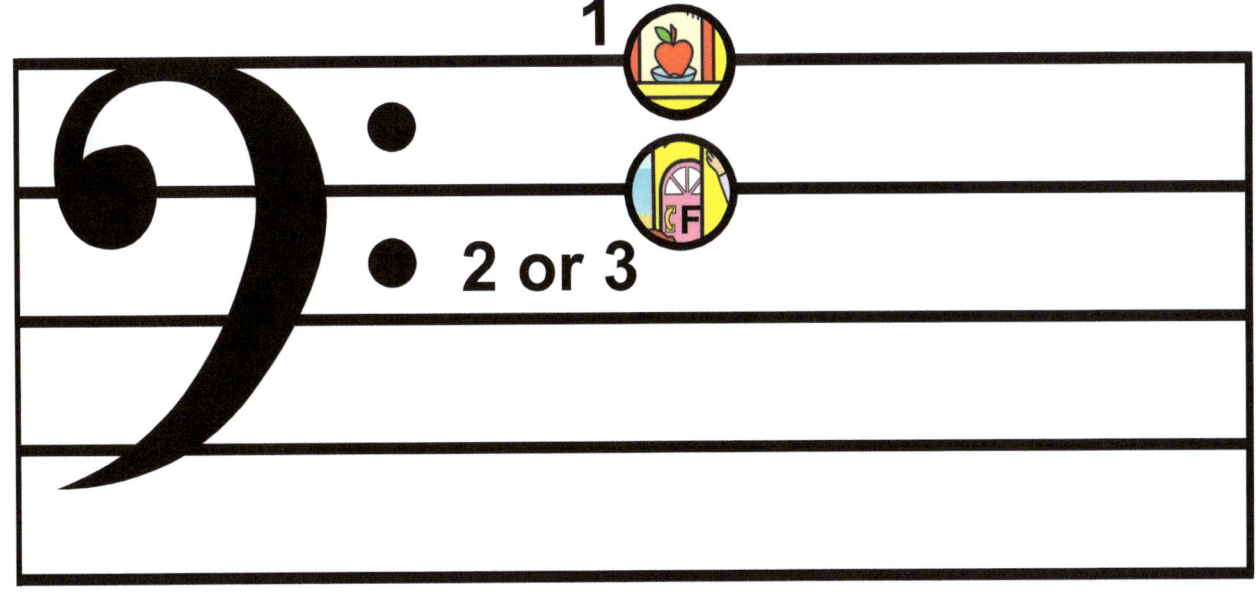

Ode to Joy

BEETHOVEN

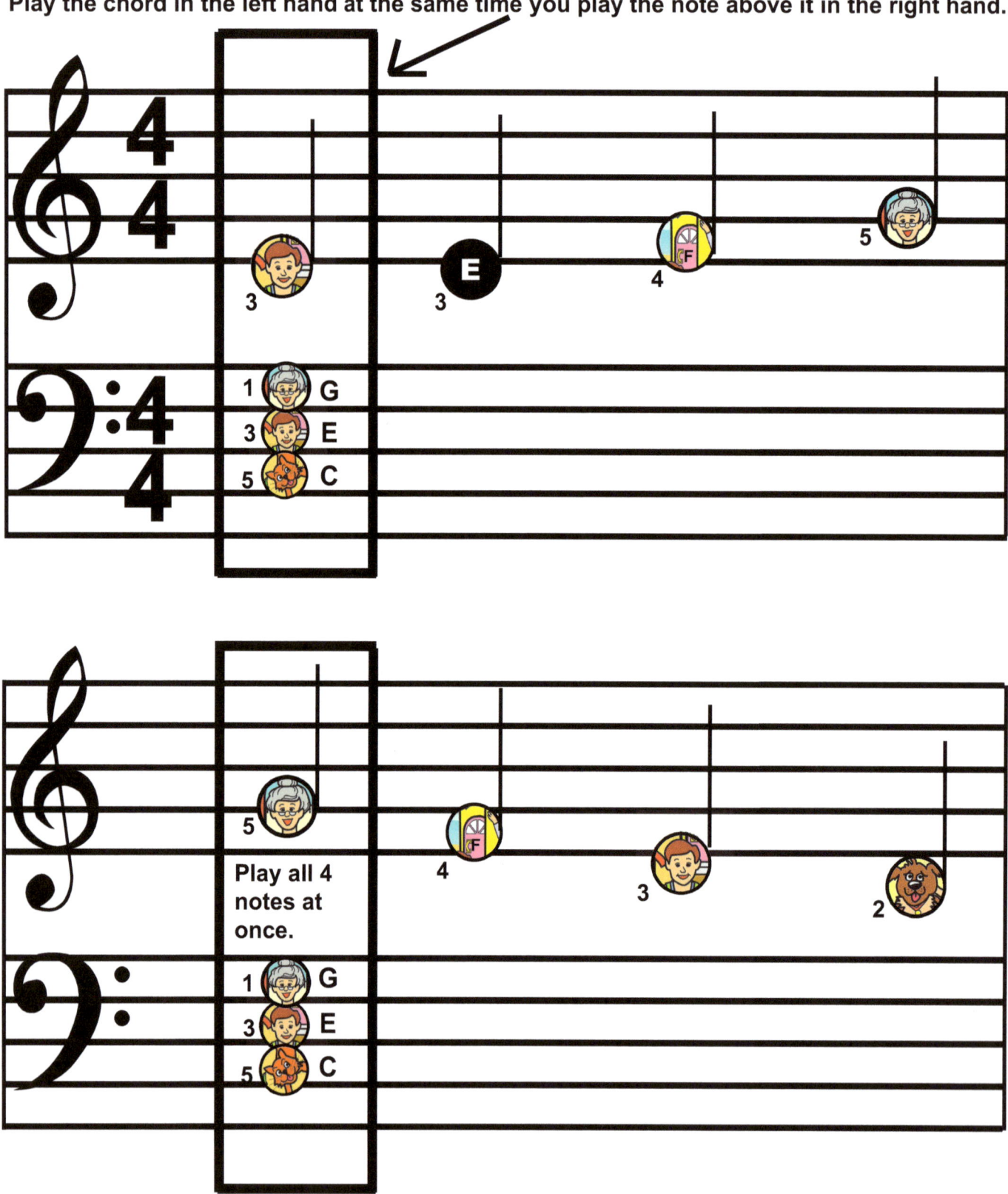

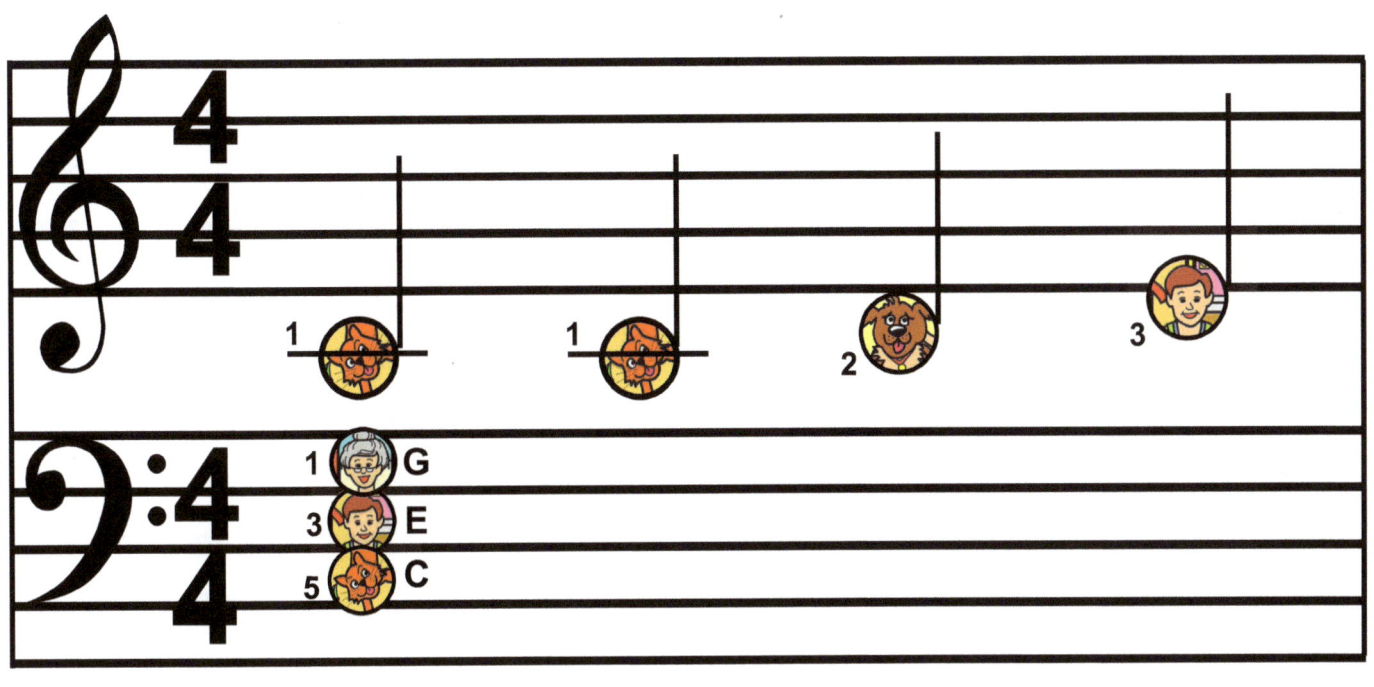
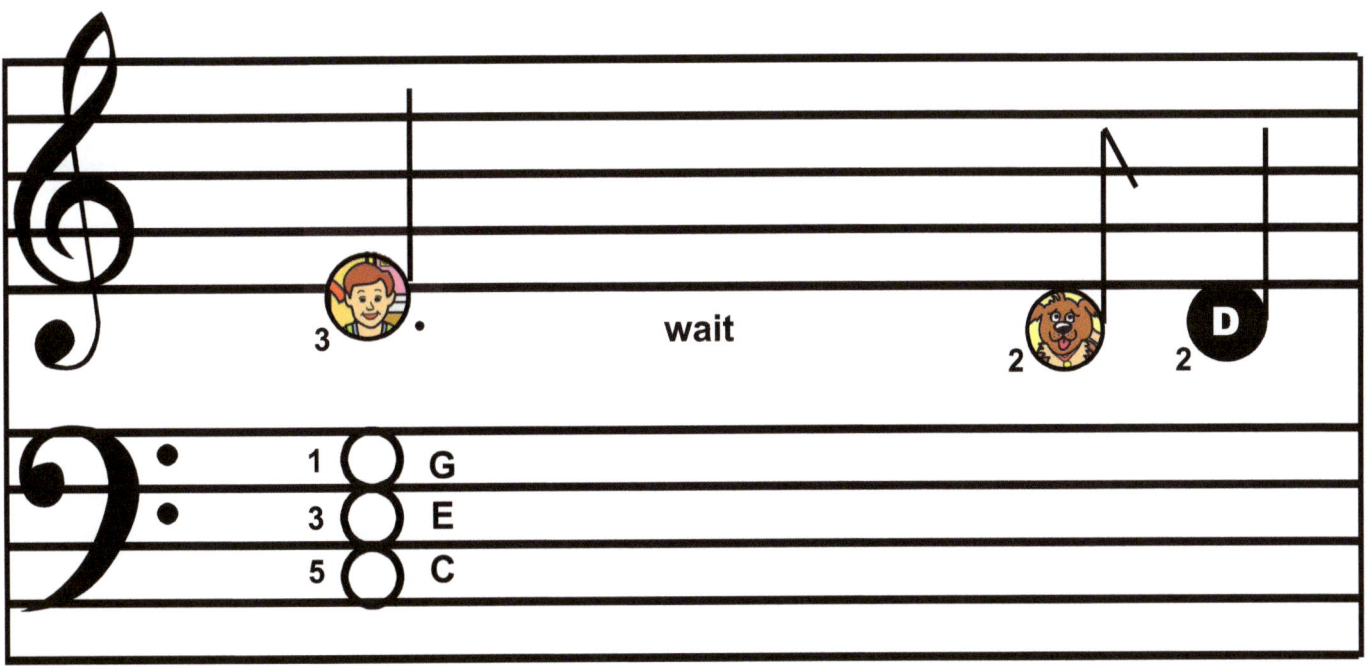

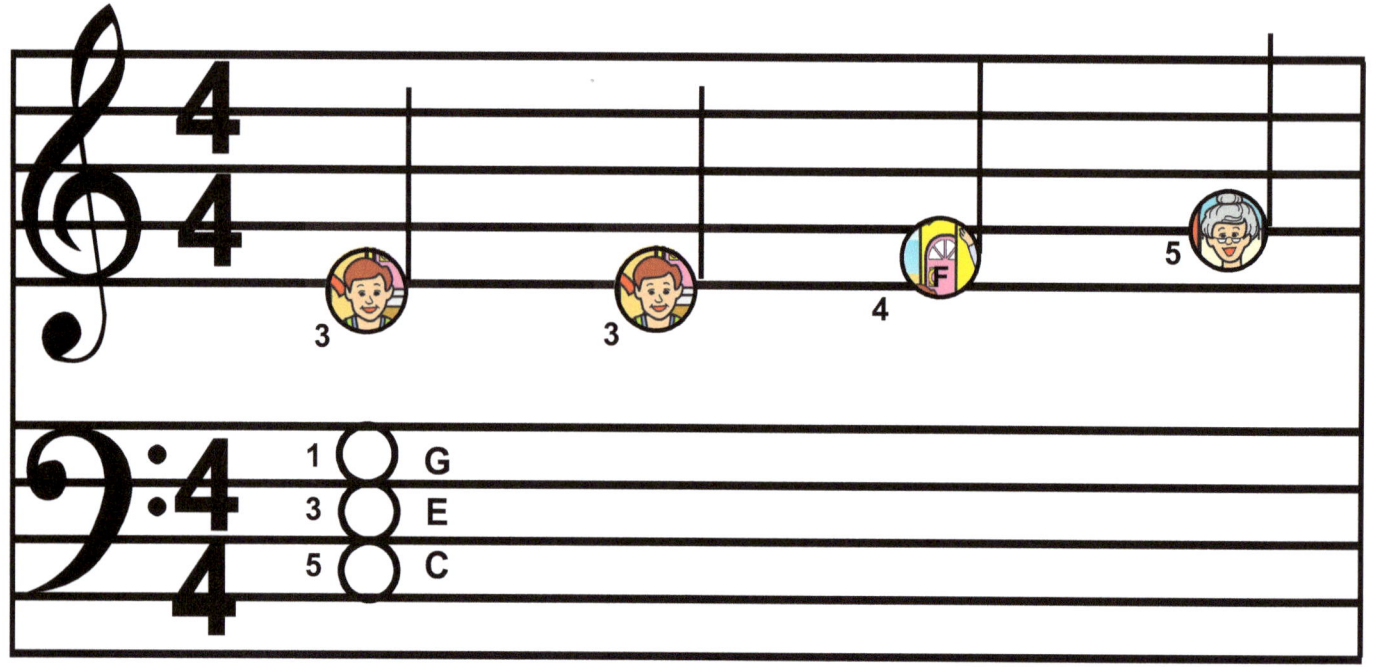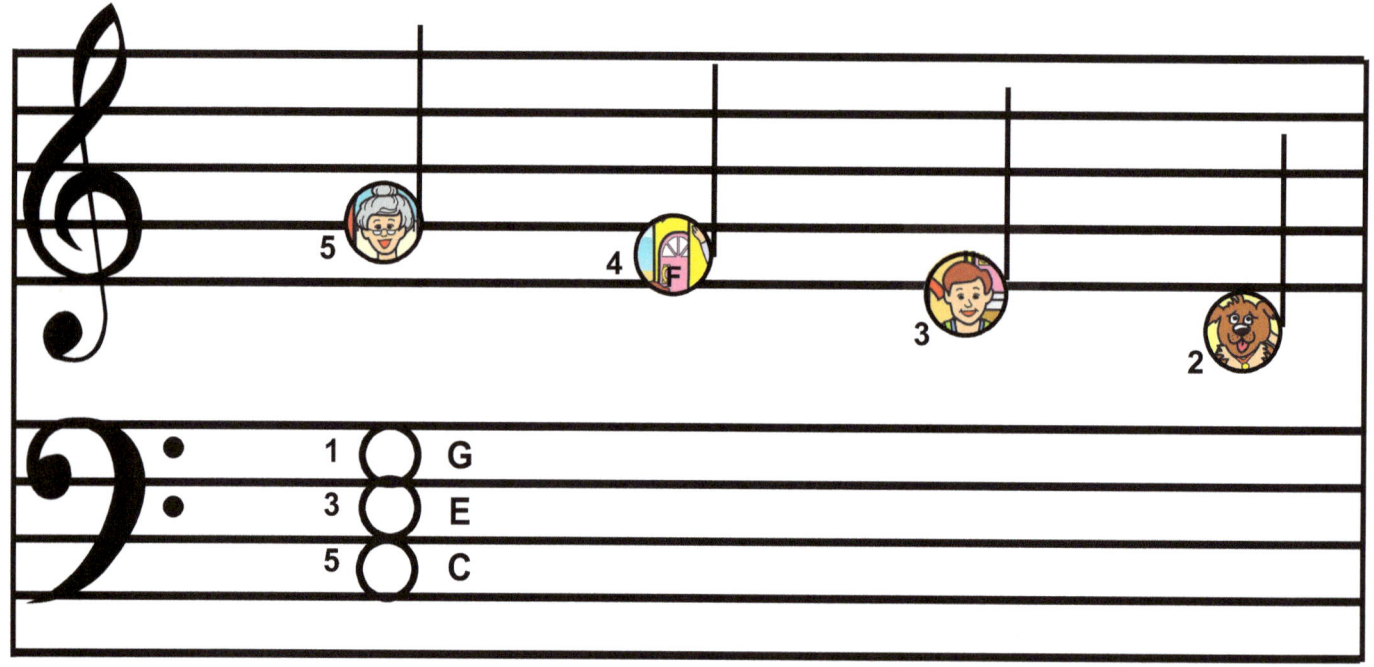

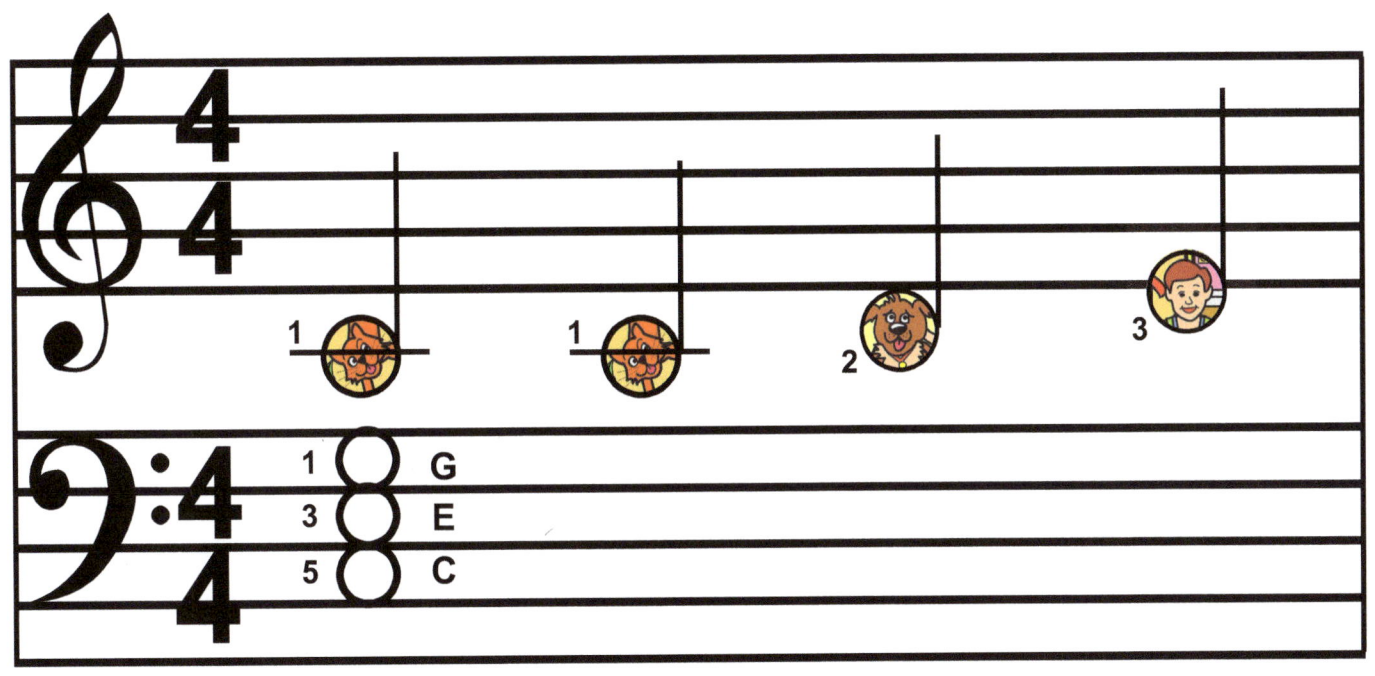

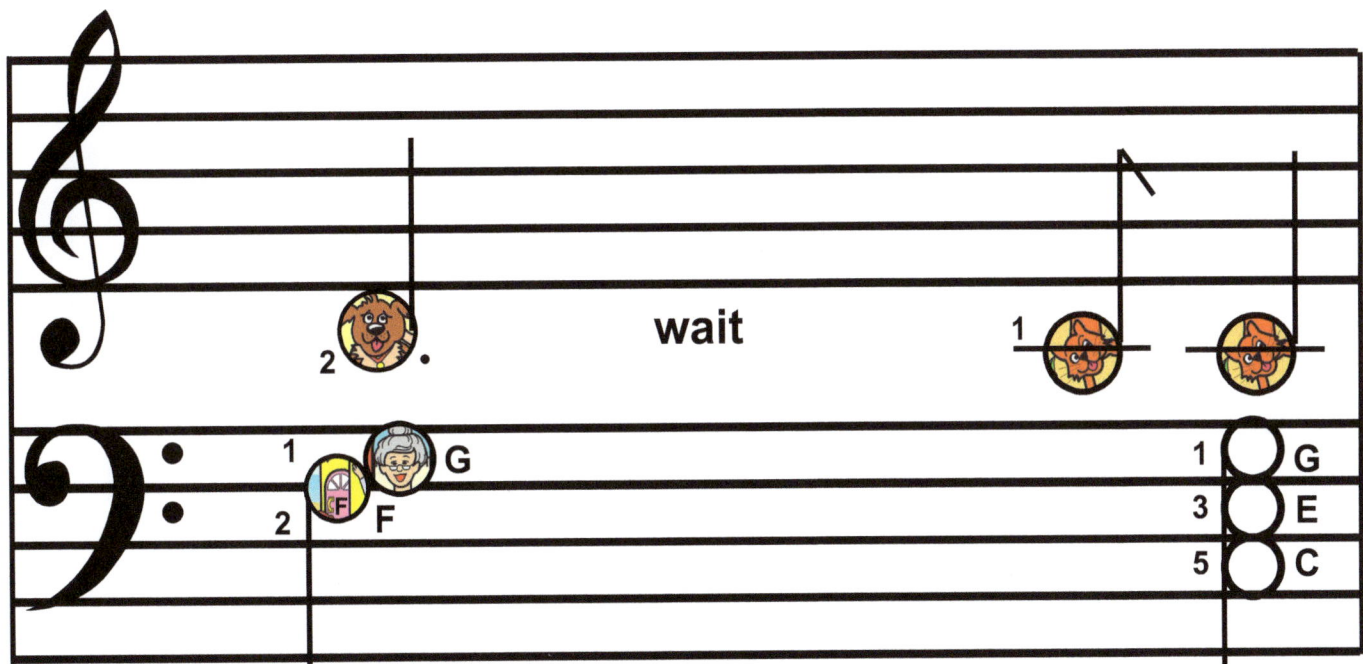

Play the F and G together to make a G7 chord, short version. Play it at the same time you play the dog in the last line of this page.

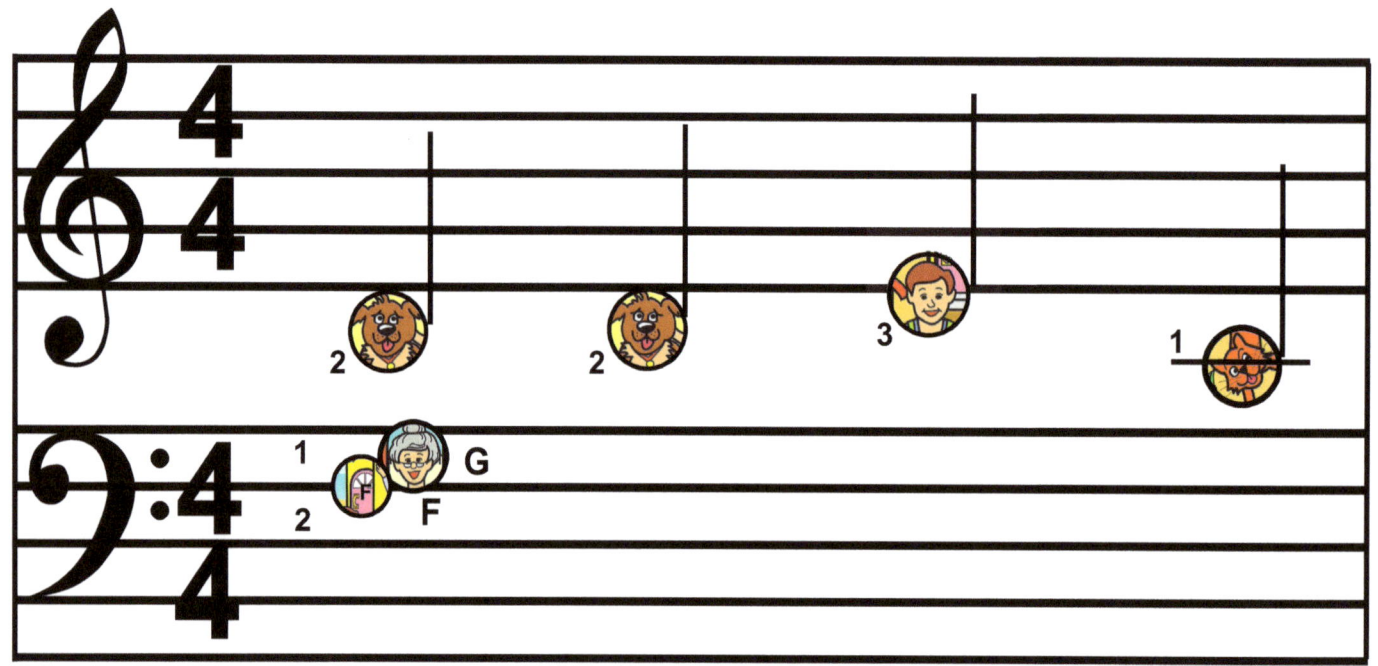

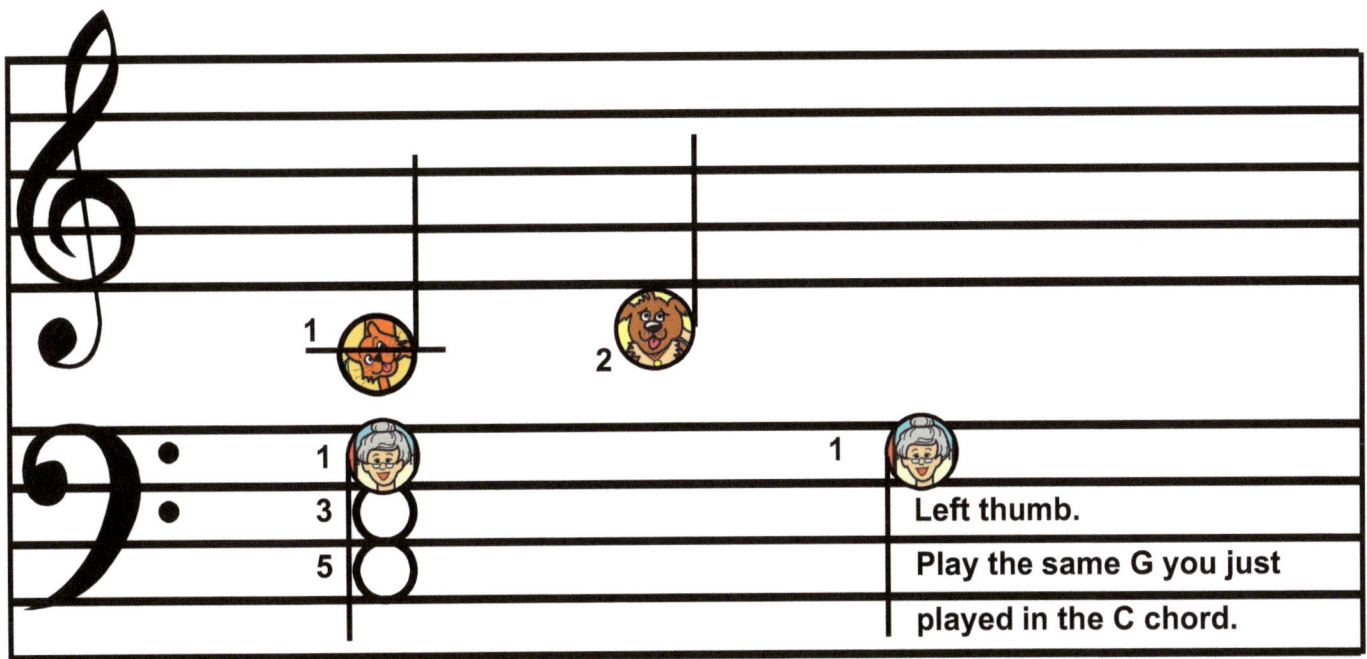

Left thumb.
Play the same G you just played in the C chord.

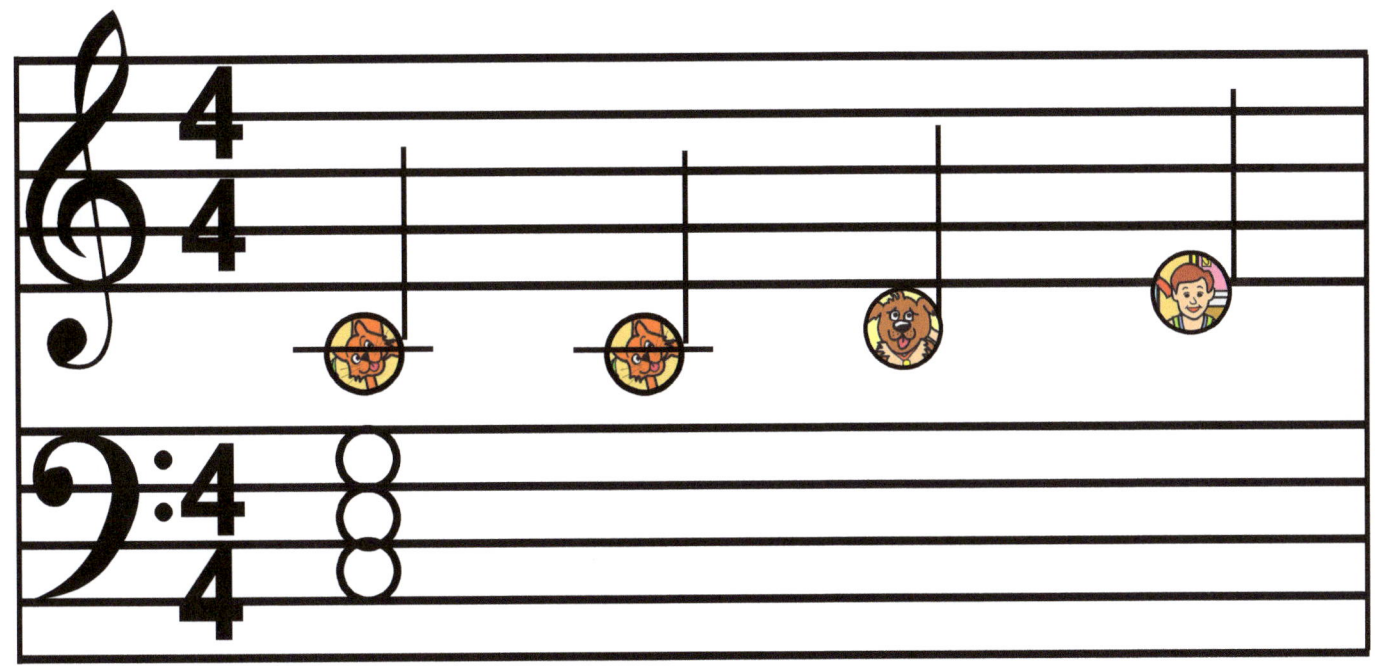
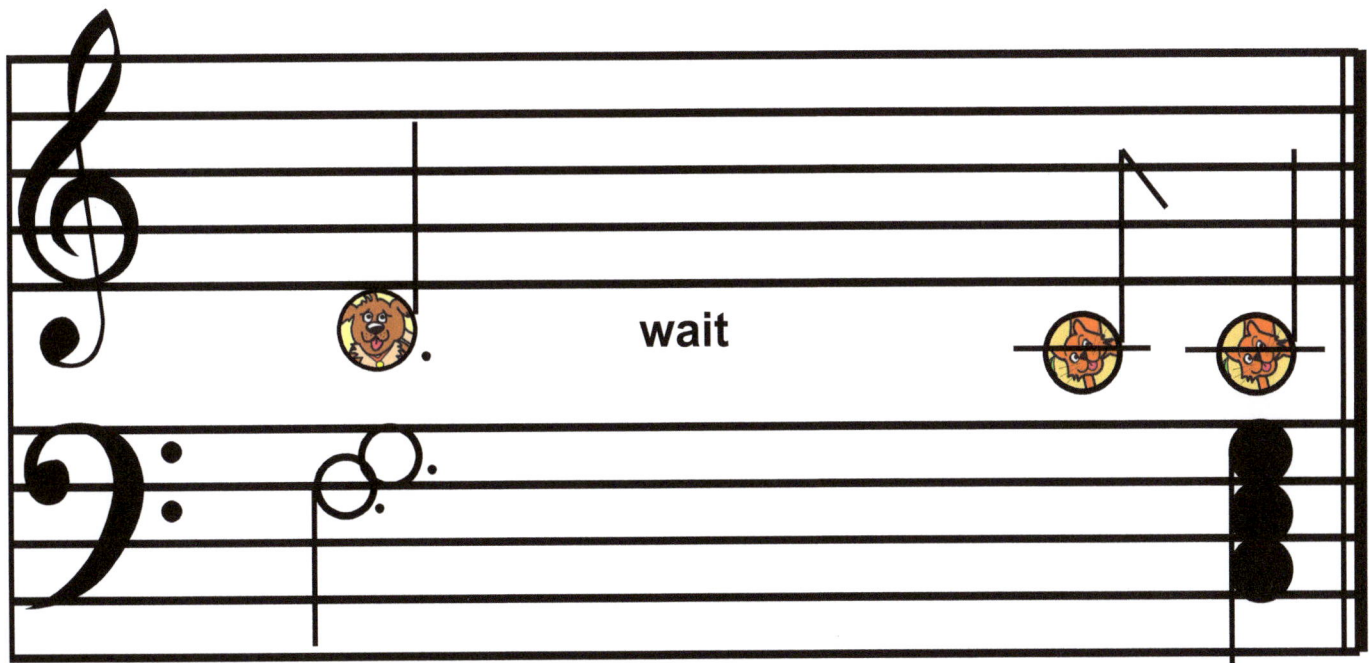

Did you notice I started to leave out a few letters and numbers? I hope you were able to play the piece without them.

GET READY FOR THE NEXT SONG

Make sure you put your Back Door B block on your piano like this for the next song in this book. The next song is Eine Kleine Nachtmusik or A Little Night Music by Mozart. You will be moving your left thumb back and forth from G to B. Practice that on the next page.

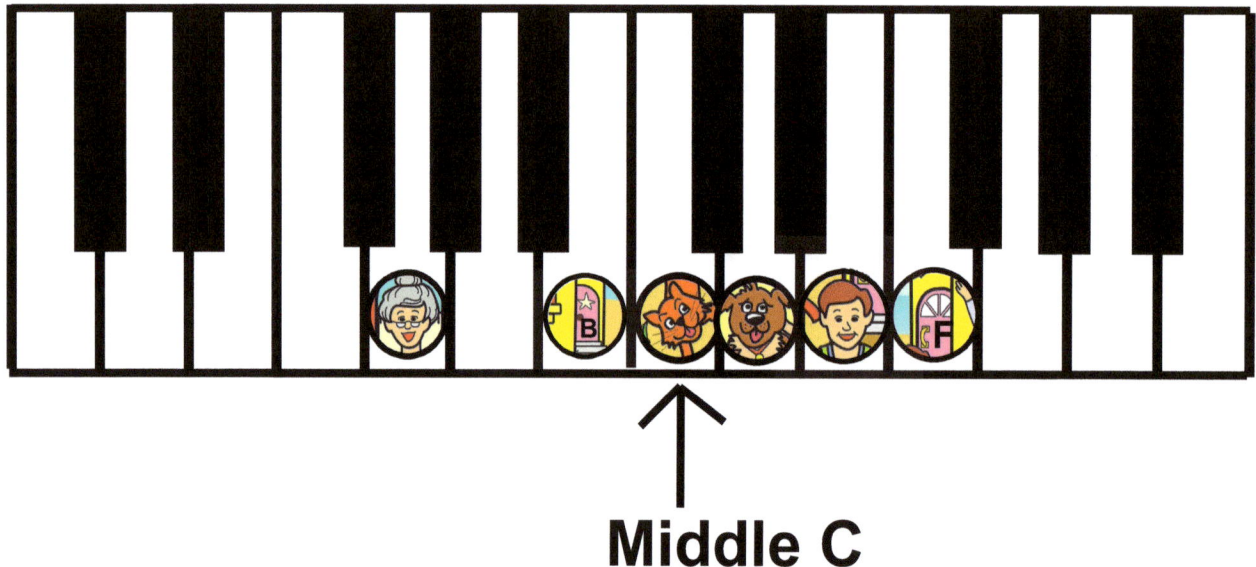

Middle C

MOVING YOUR FINGERS

Now you will need to start moving your fingers around the piano keyboard for new songs. Practice moving your left thumb (1st finger) from Grandma G to Back Door B.

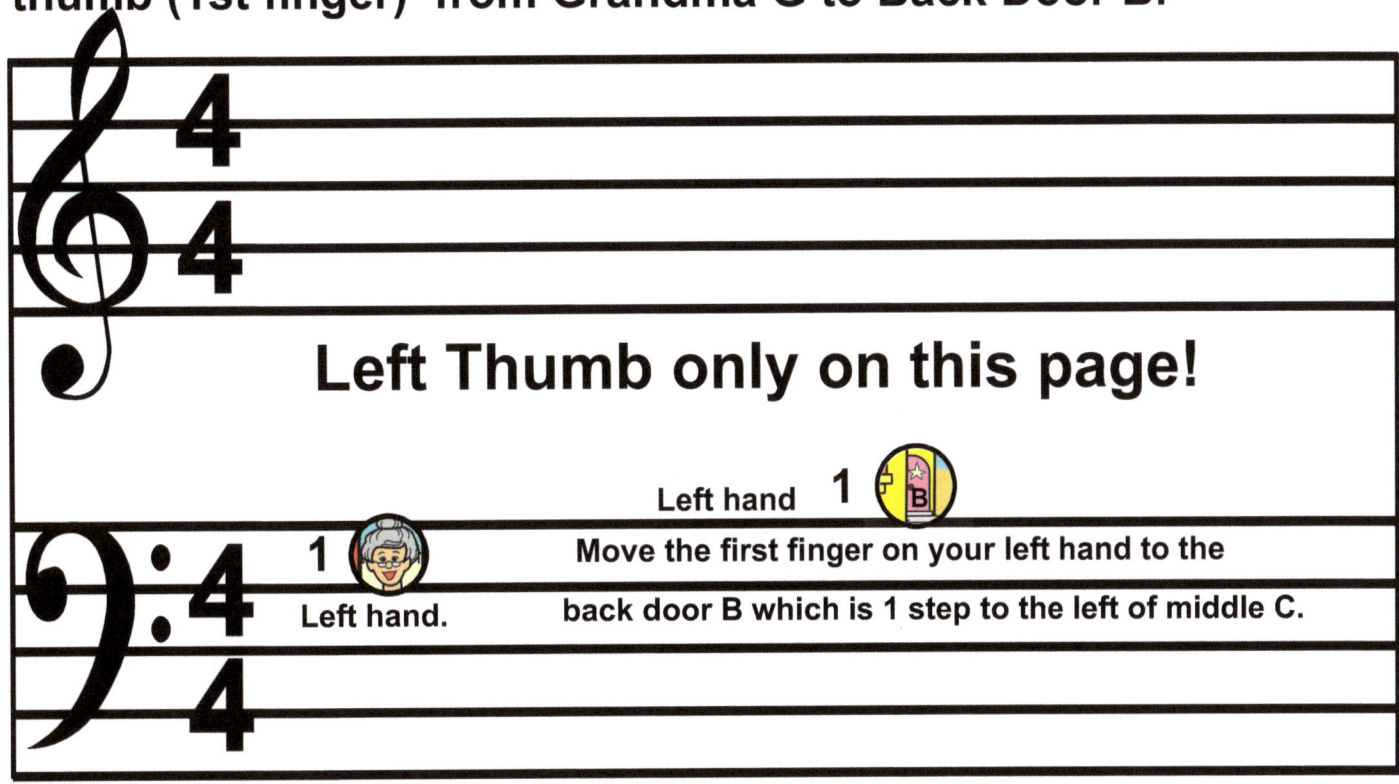

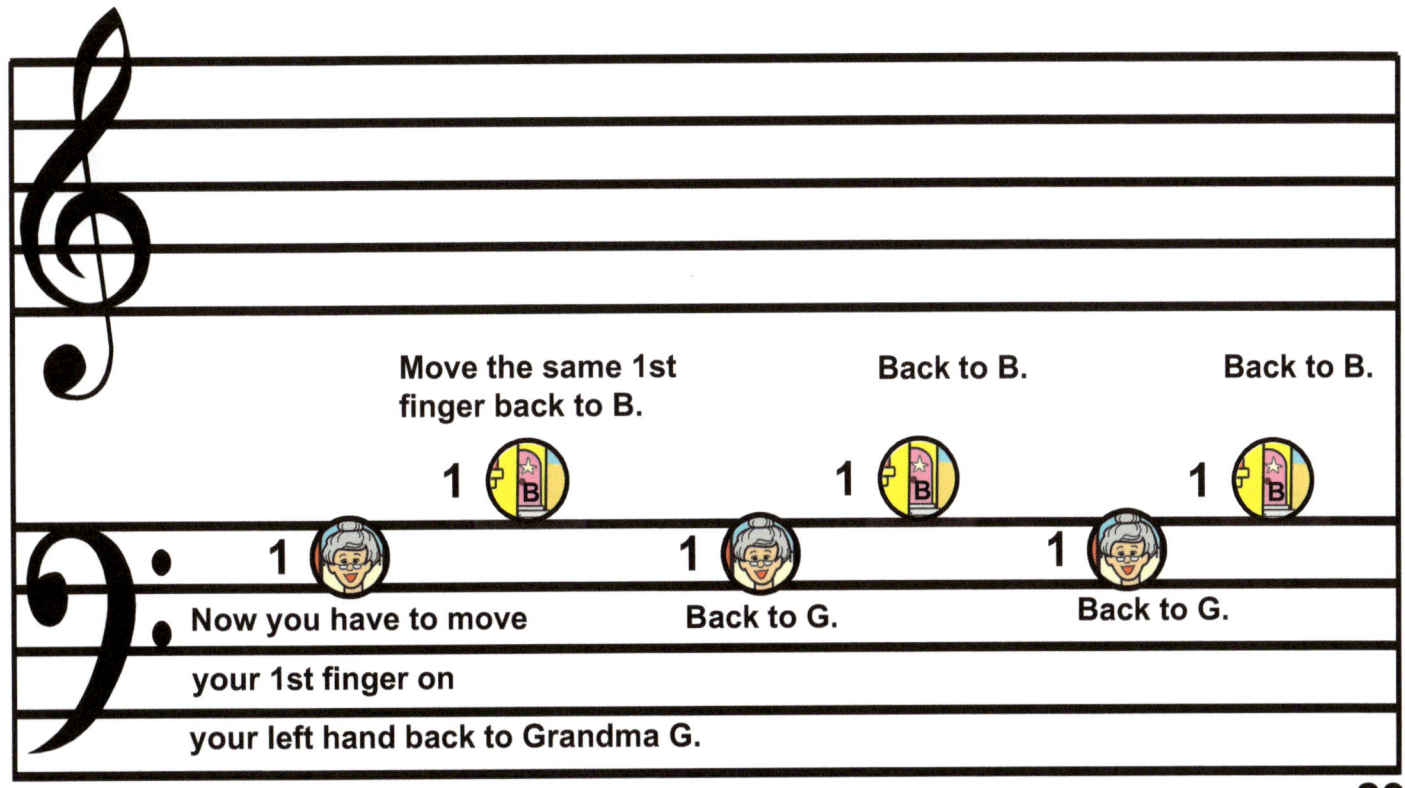

Eine Kleine Nachtmusik
A Little Night Music

Mozart

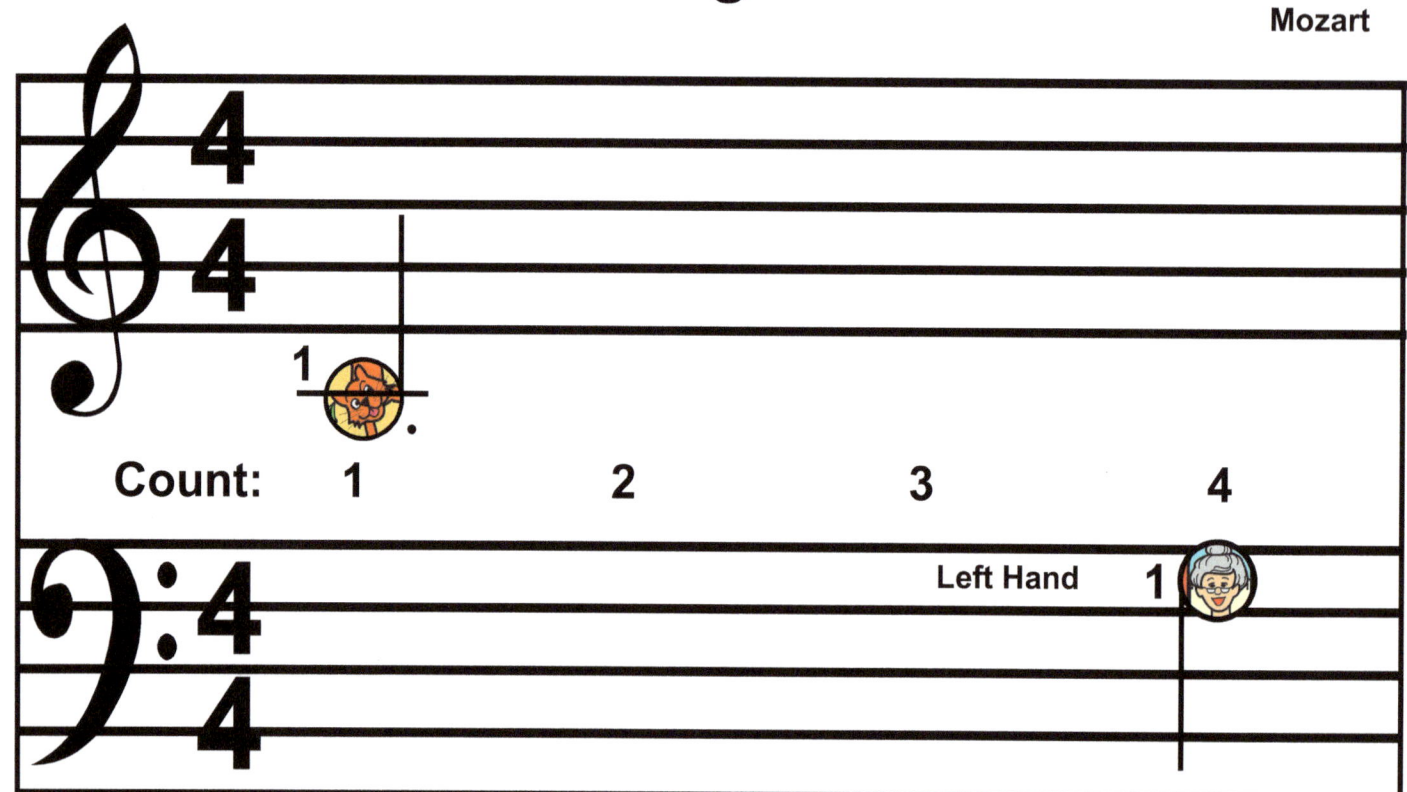

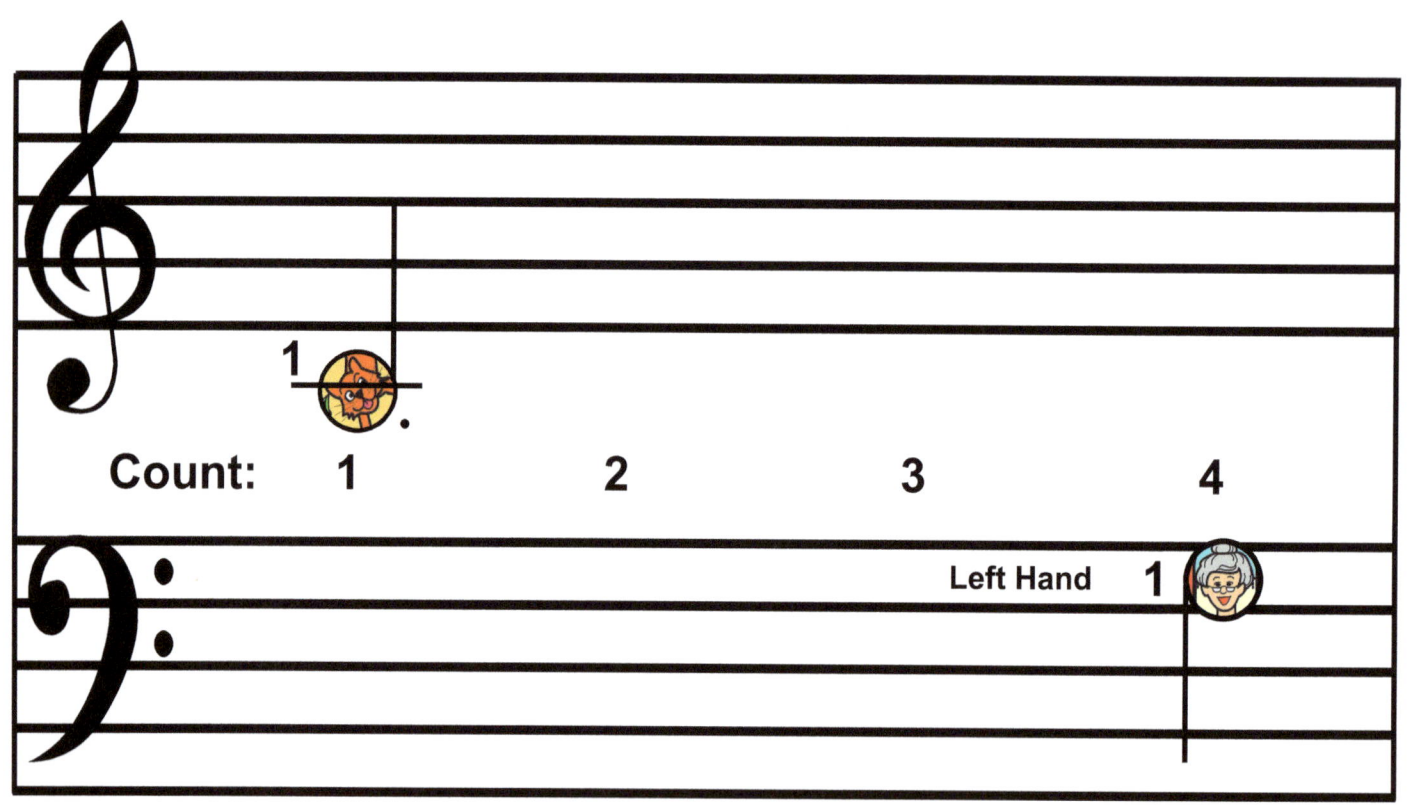

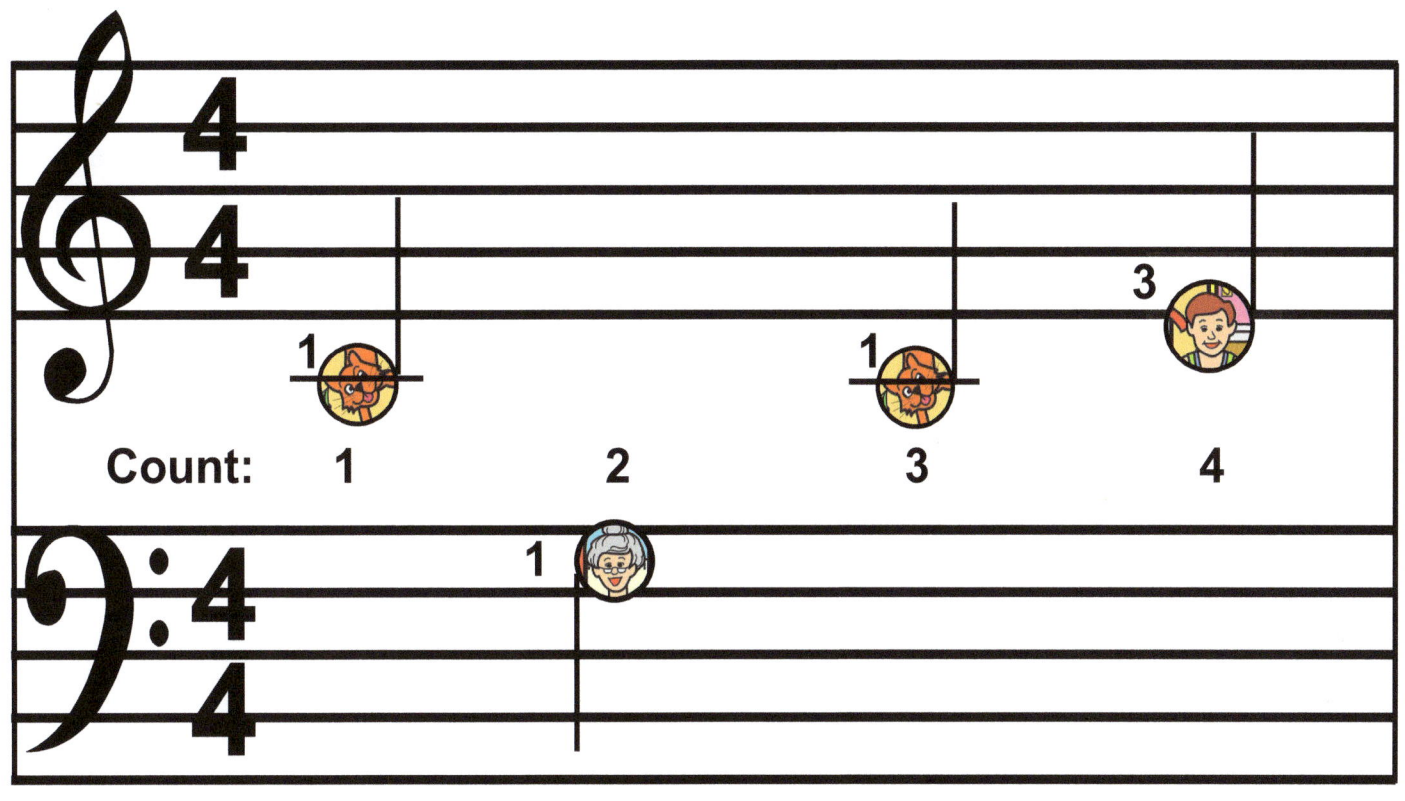
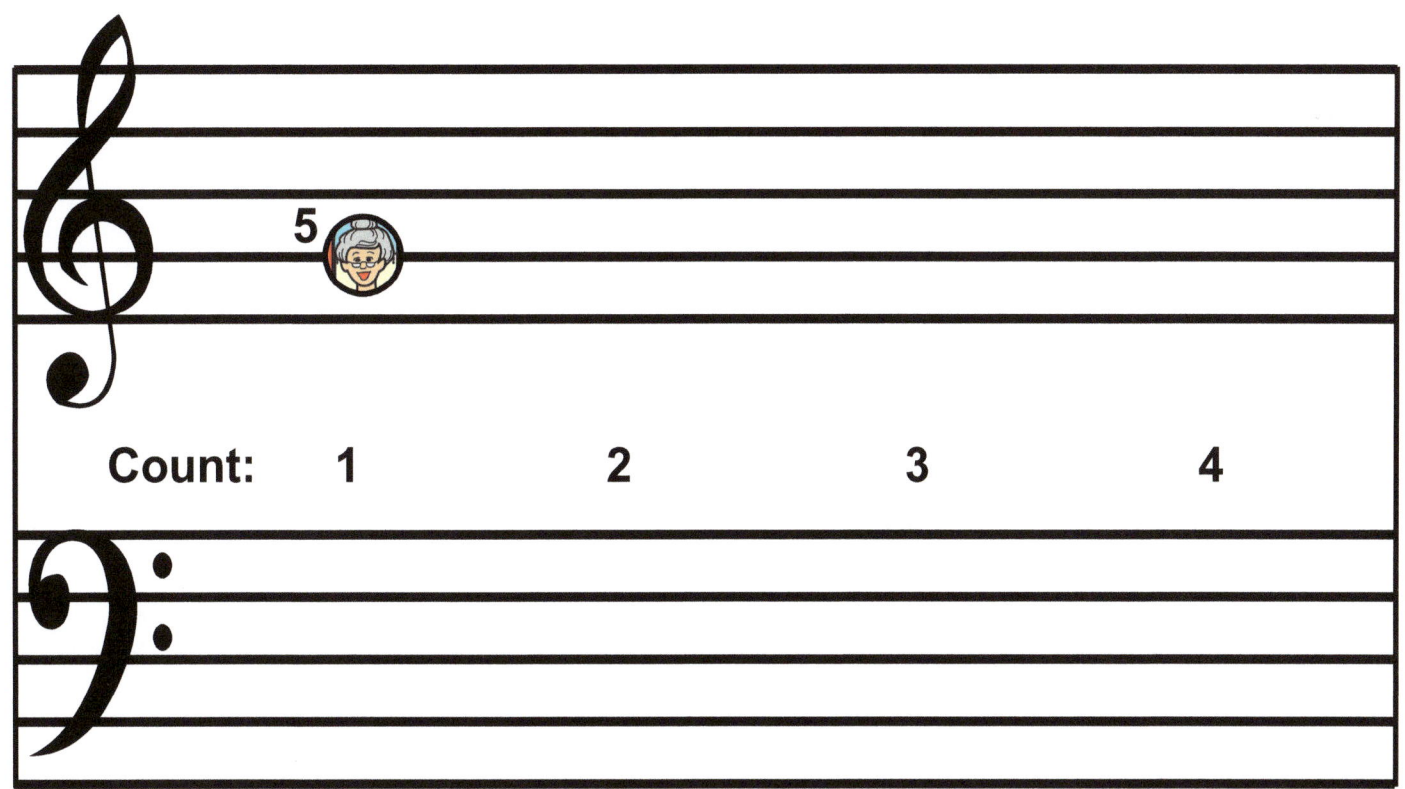

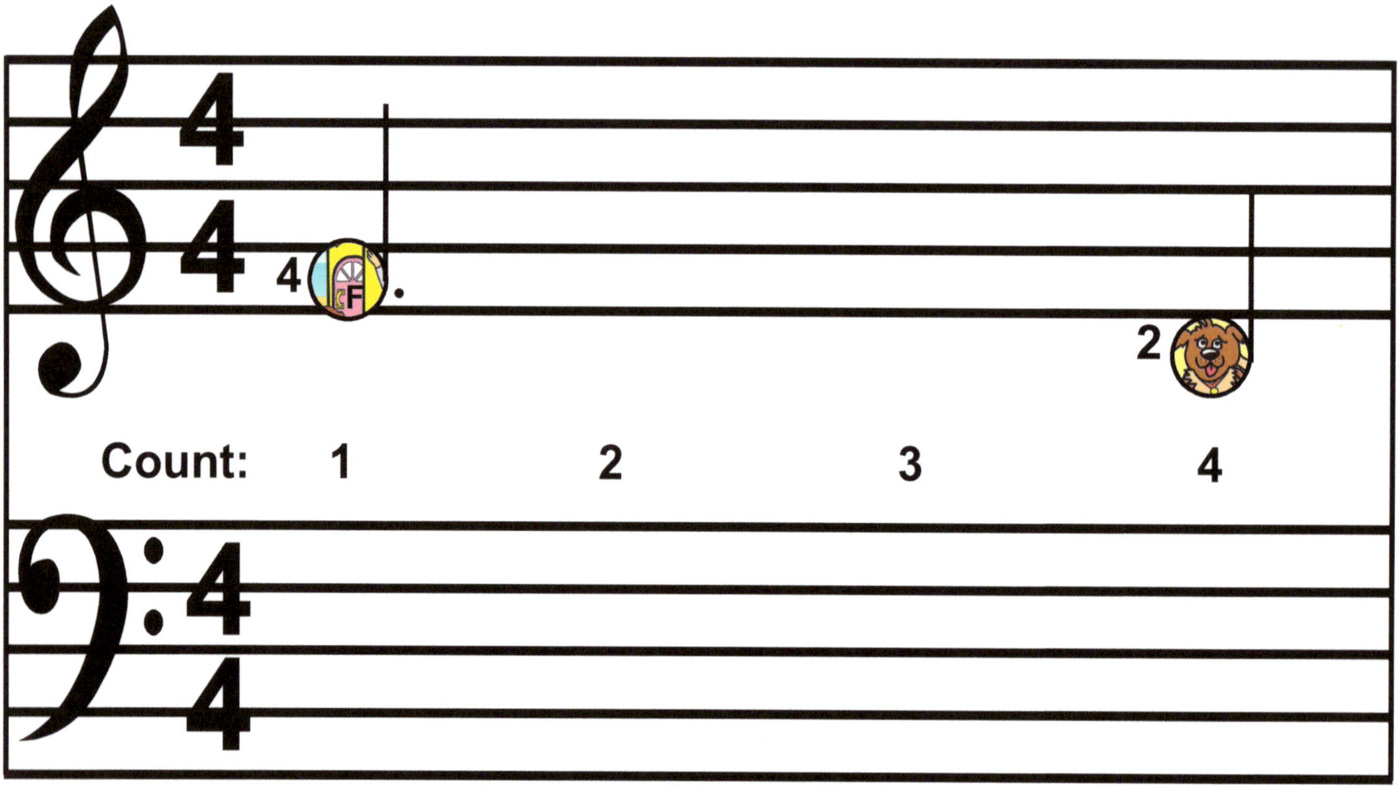

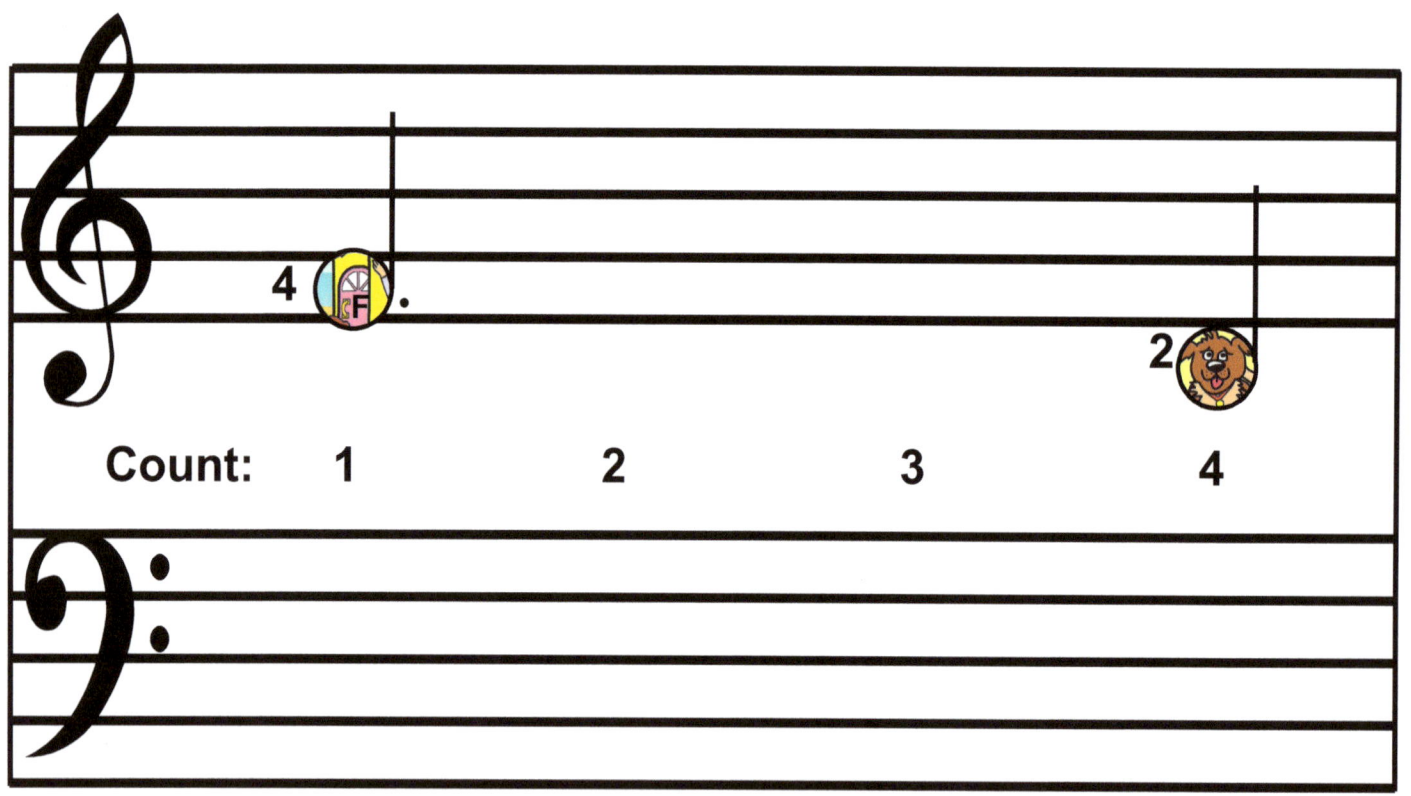

4
2
2
Count: 1 2 3 4
1
Left hand
Move the first finger on your left hand to the
back door B which is 1 step to the left of middle C.

Count: 1 2 3 4
1
Now you have to move the first finger on
your left hand back to Grandma G.

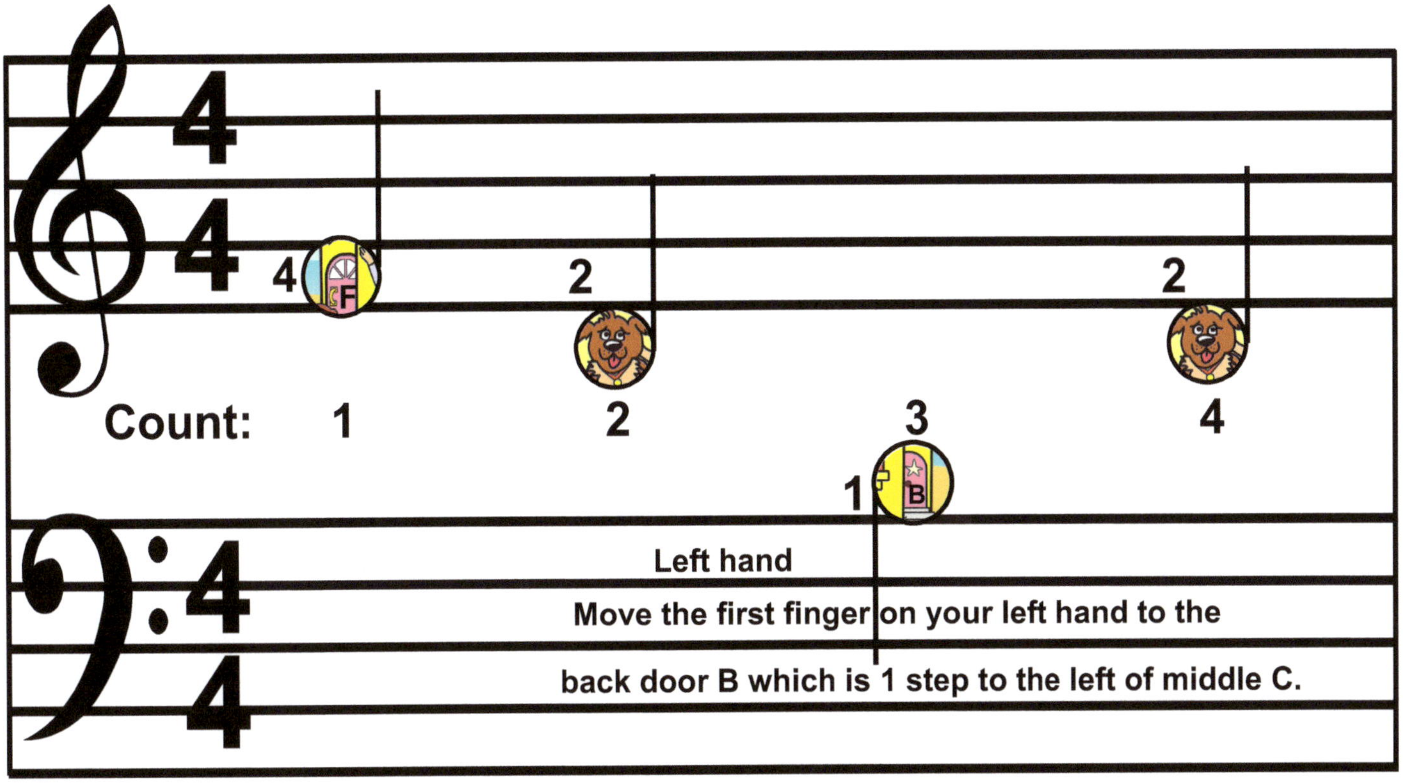

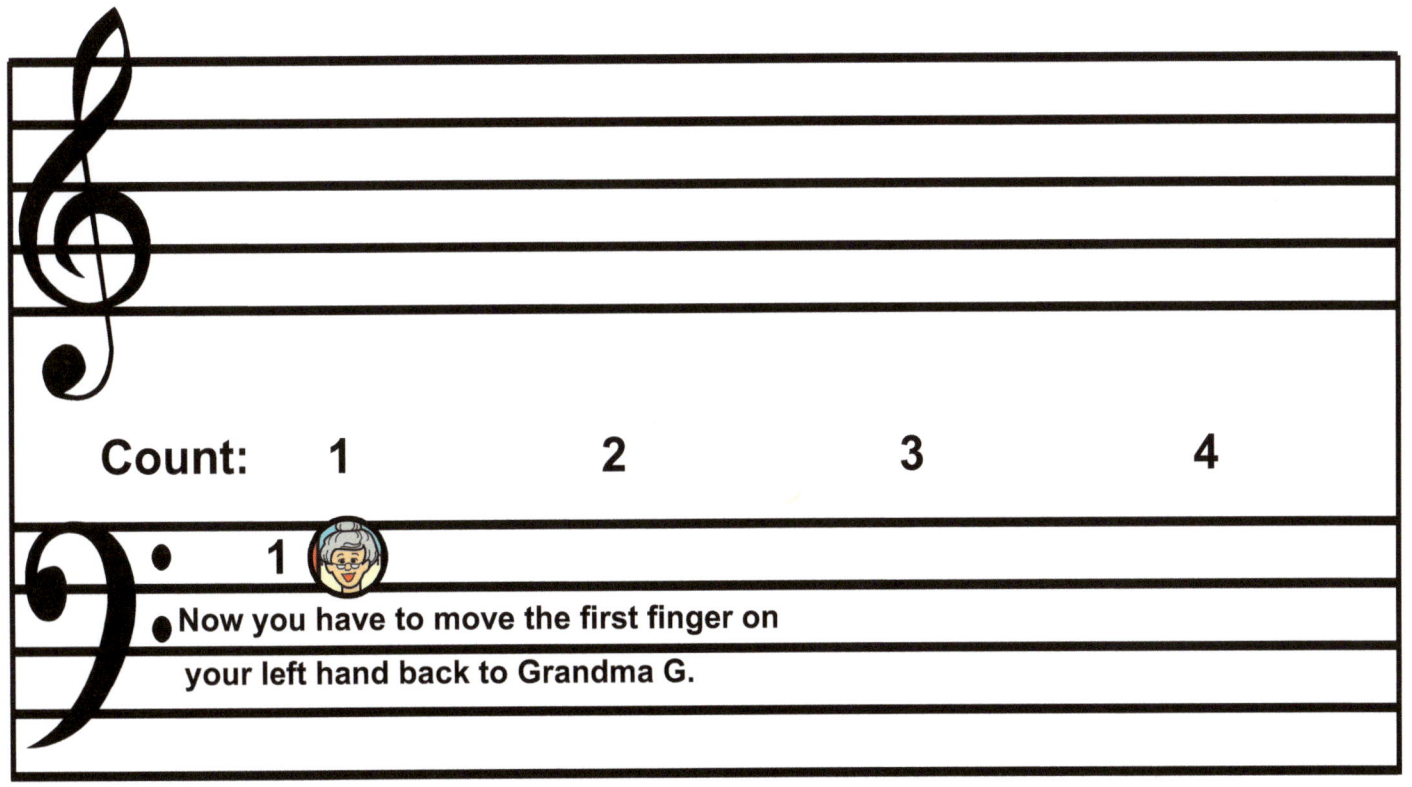

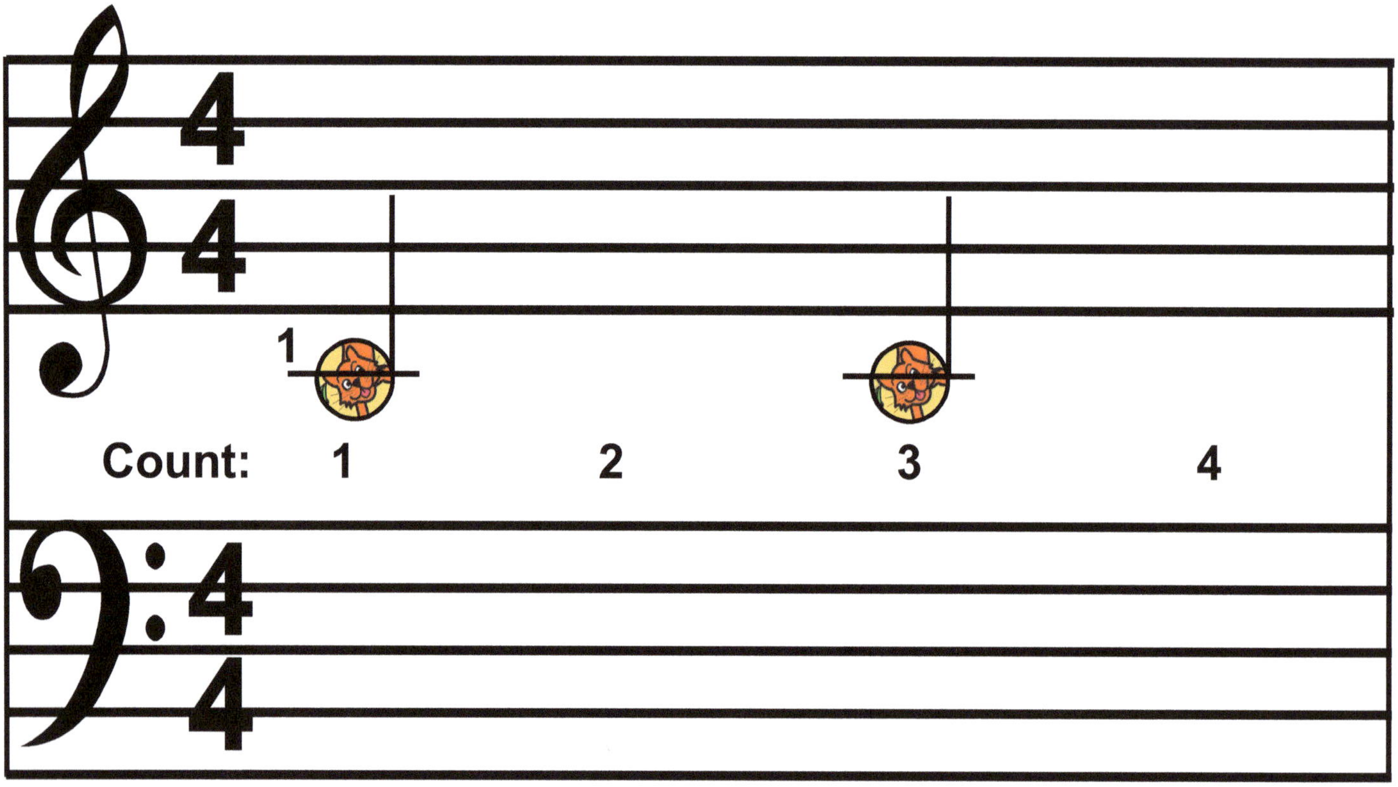

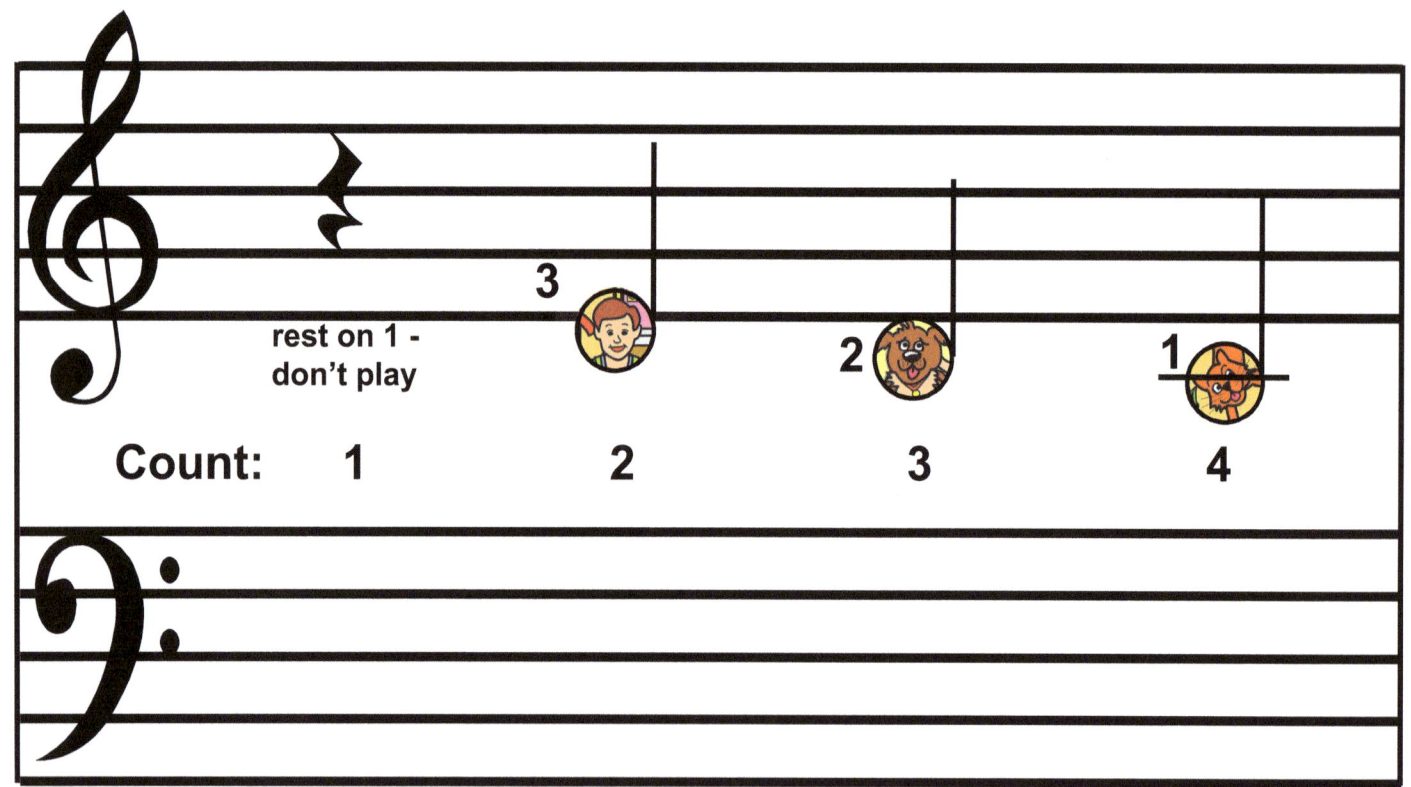

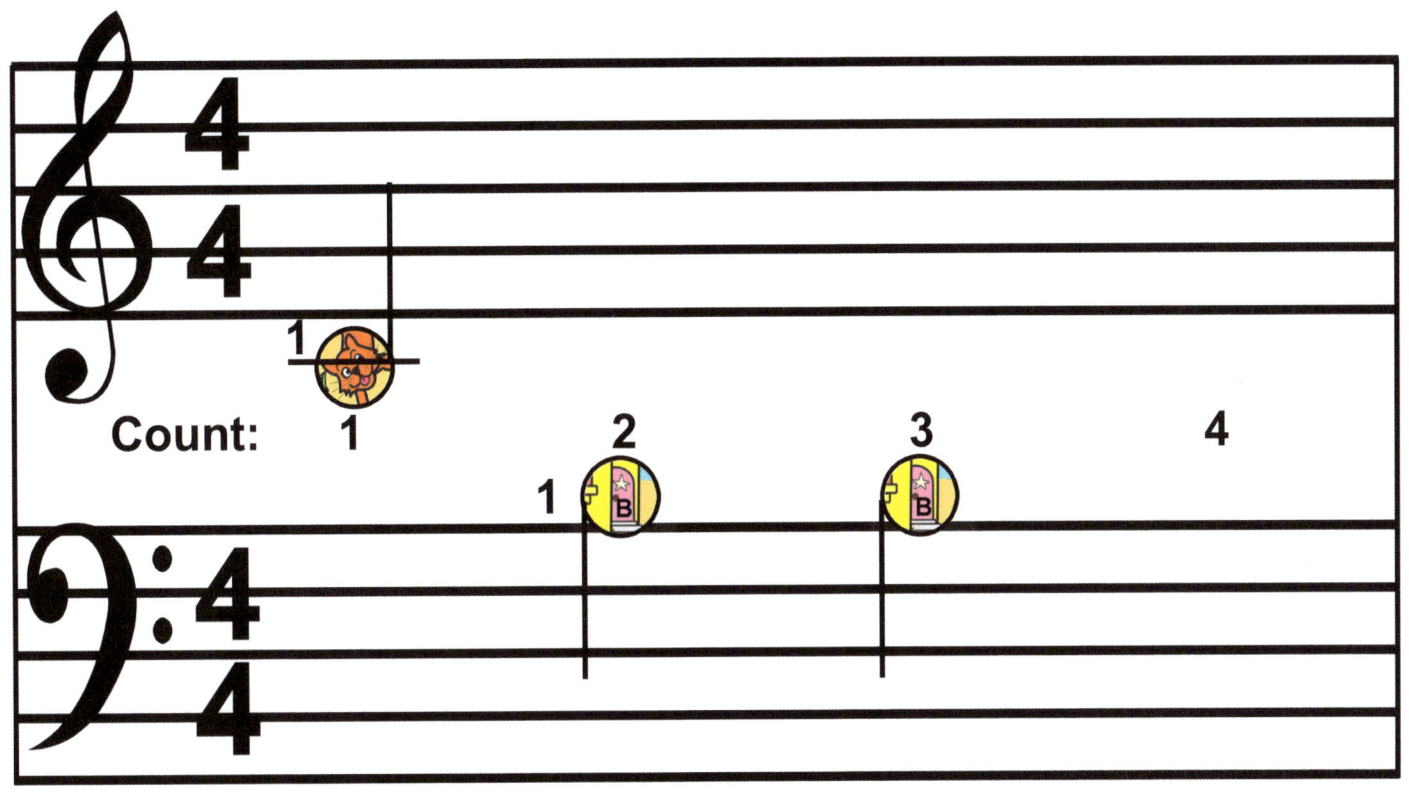
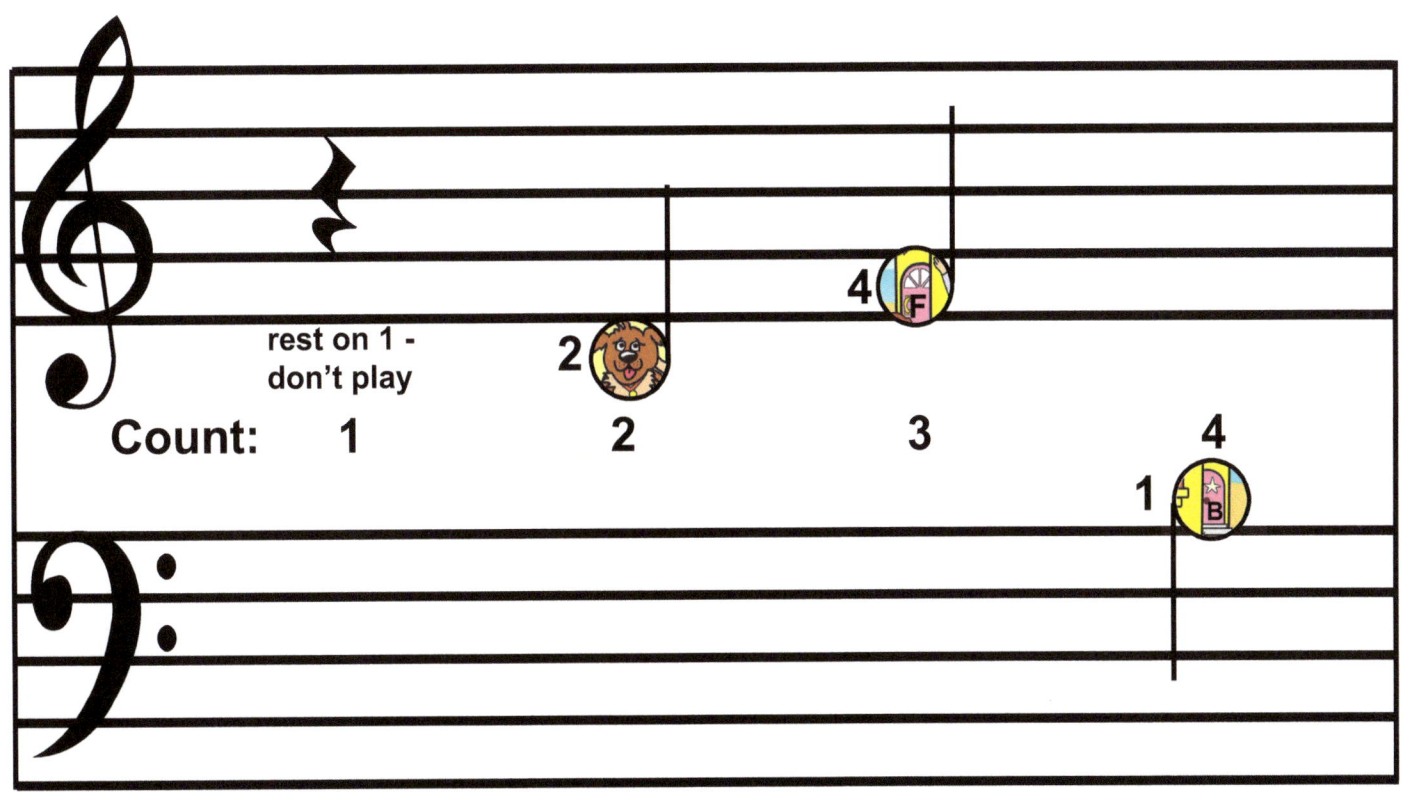

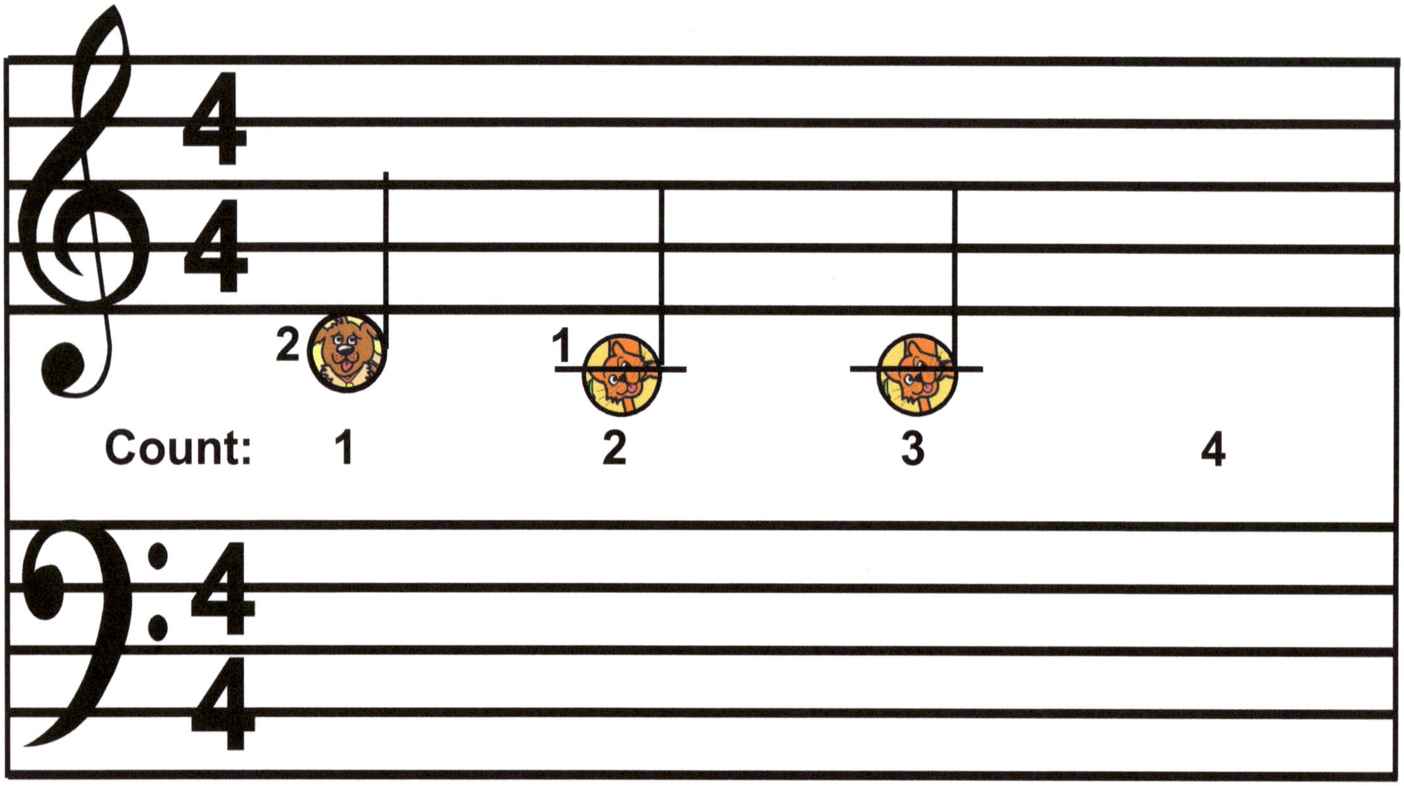

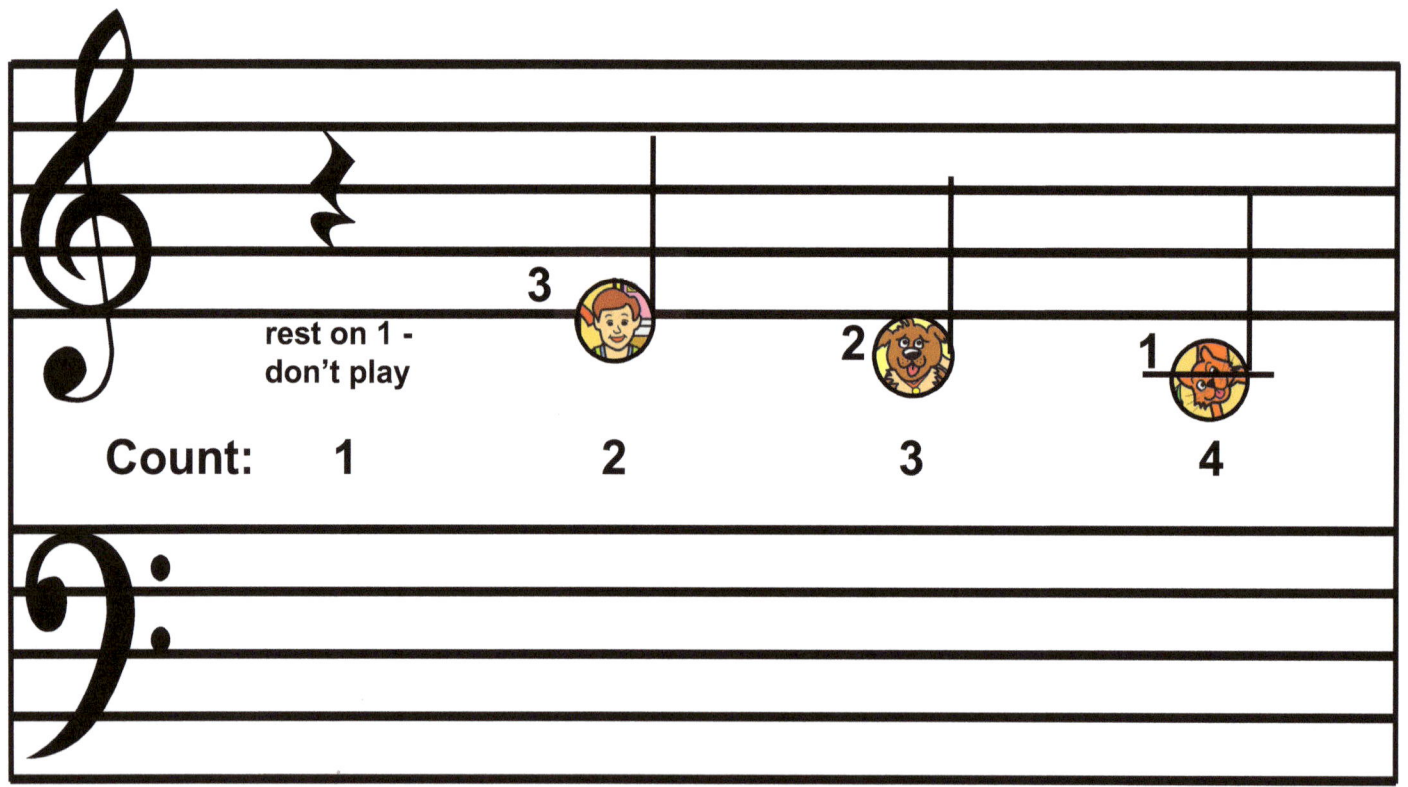

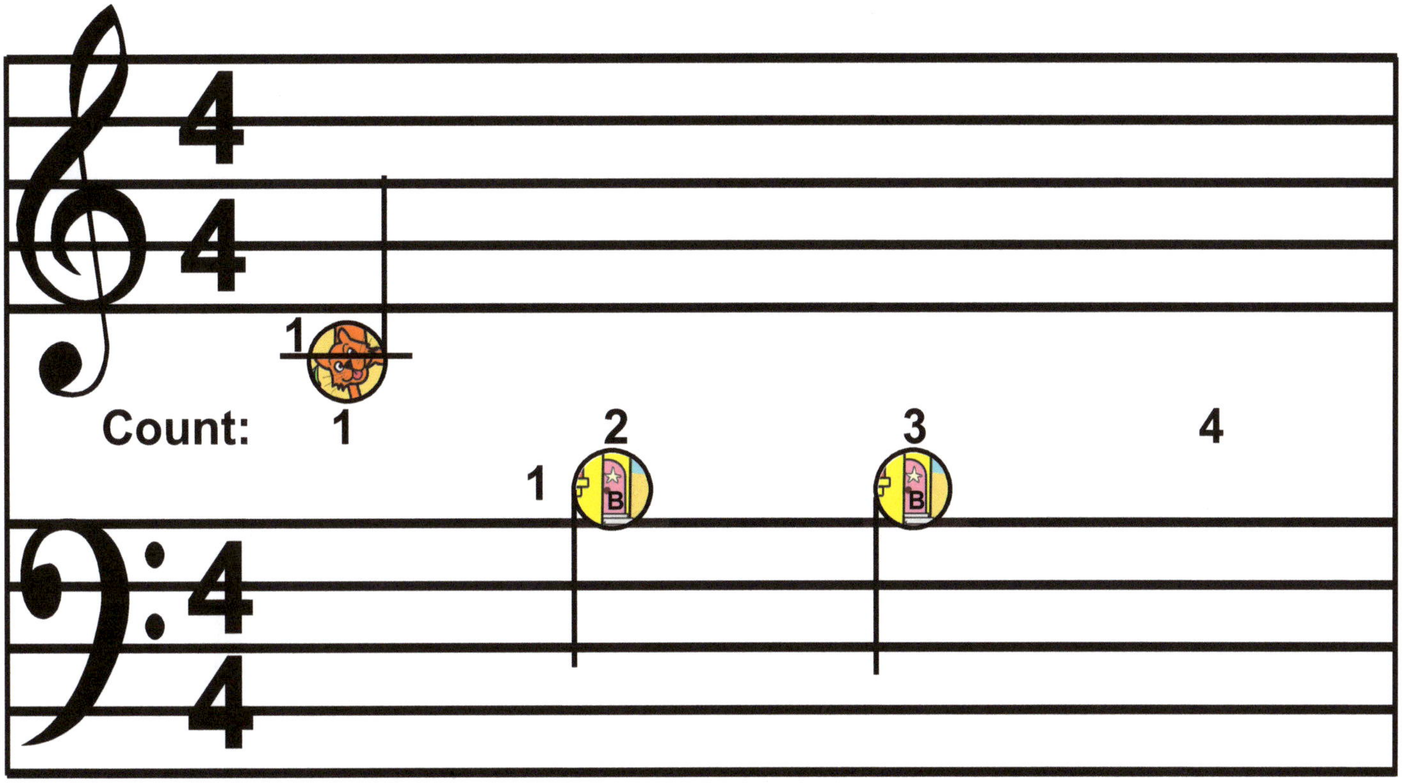
1
Count: 1 2 3 4
1 B
B

rest on 1 -
don't play
2
4 F
Count: 1 2 3 4
1 B

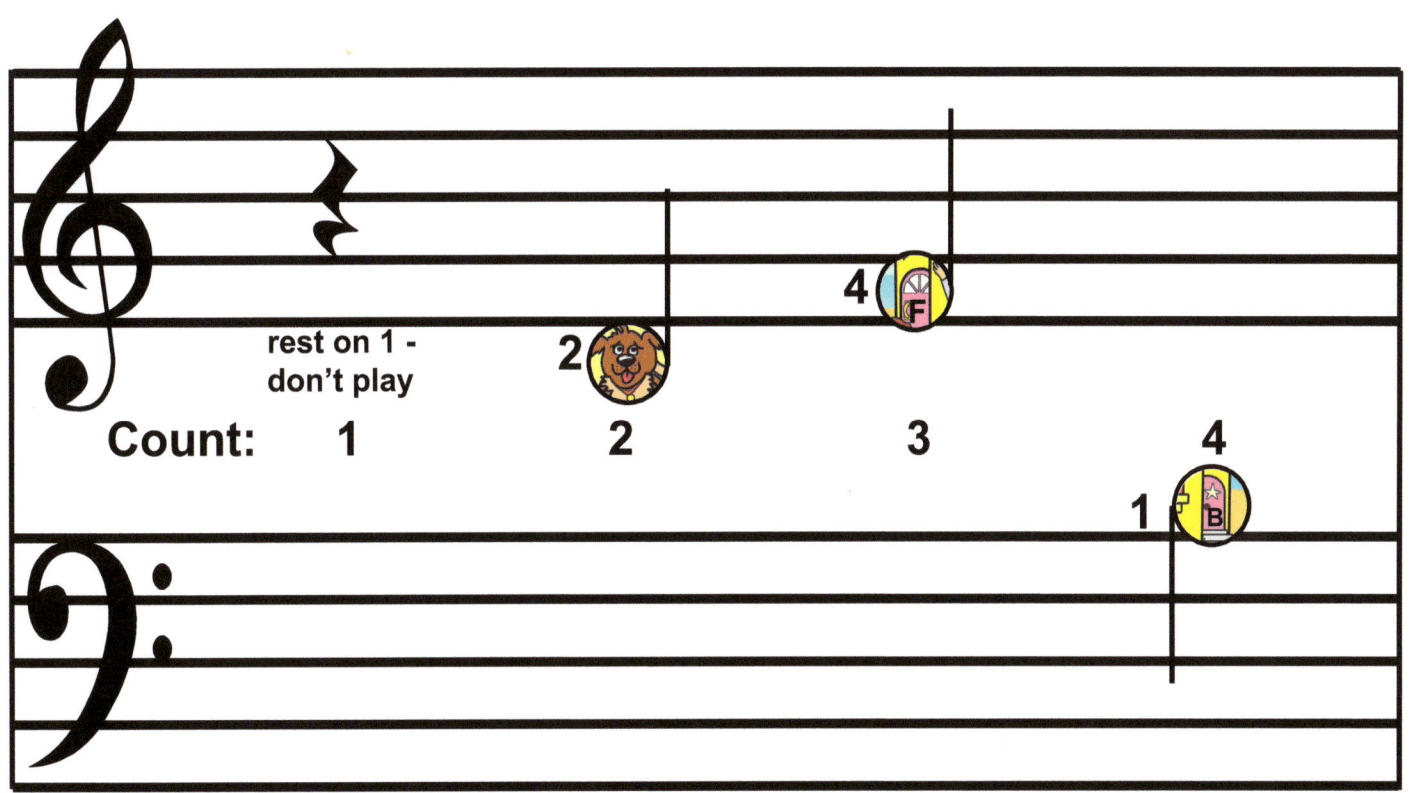

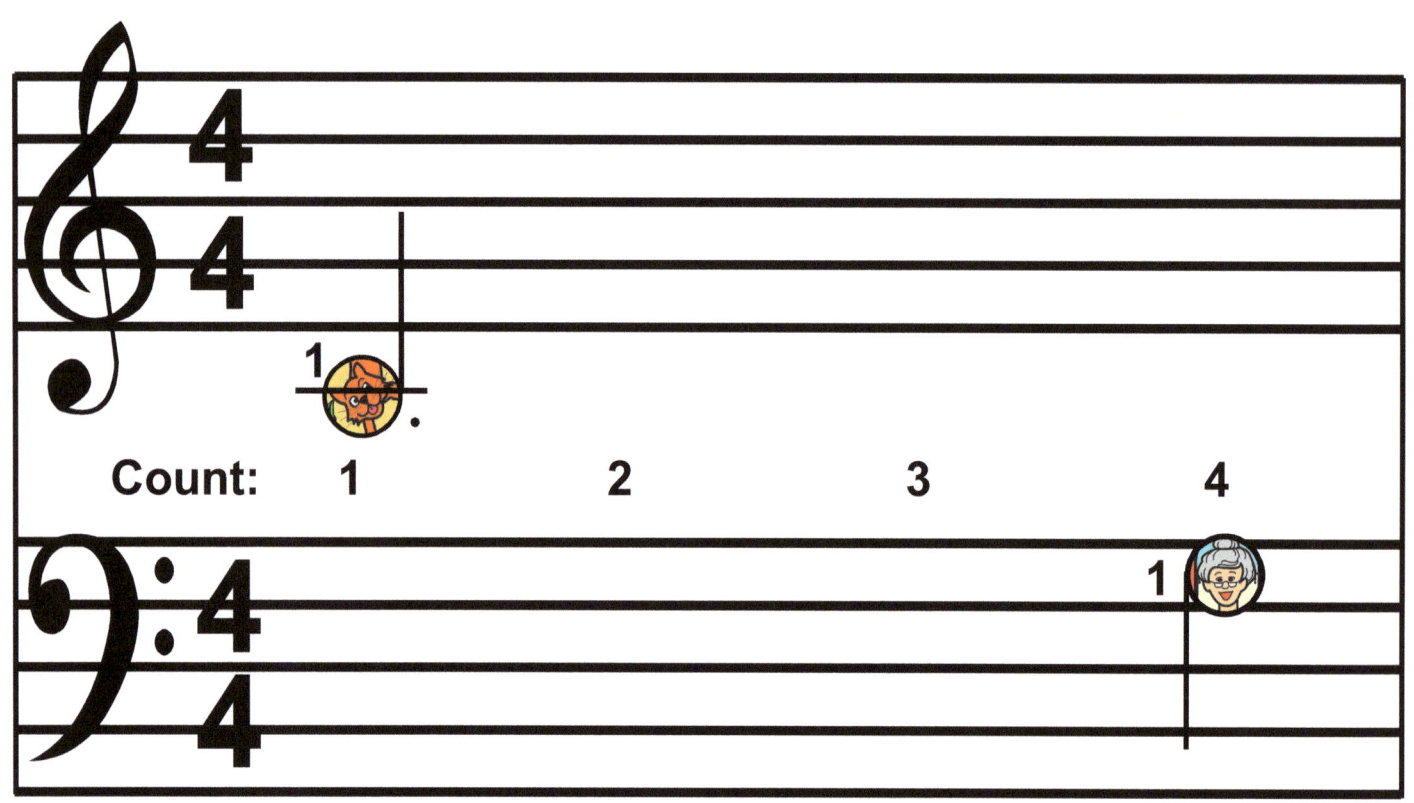
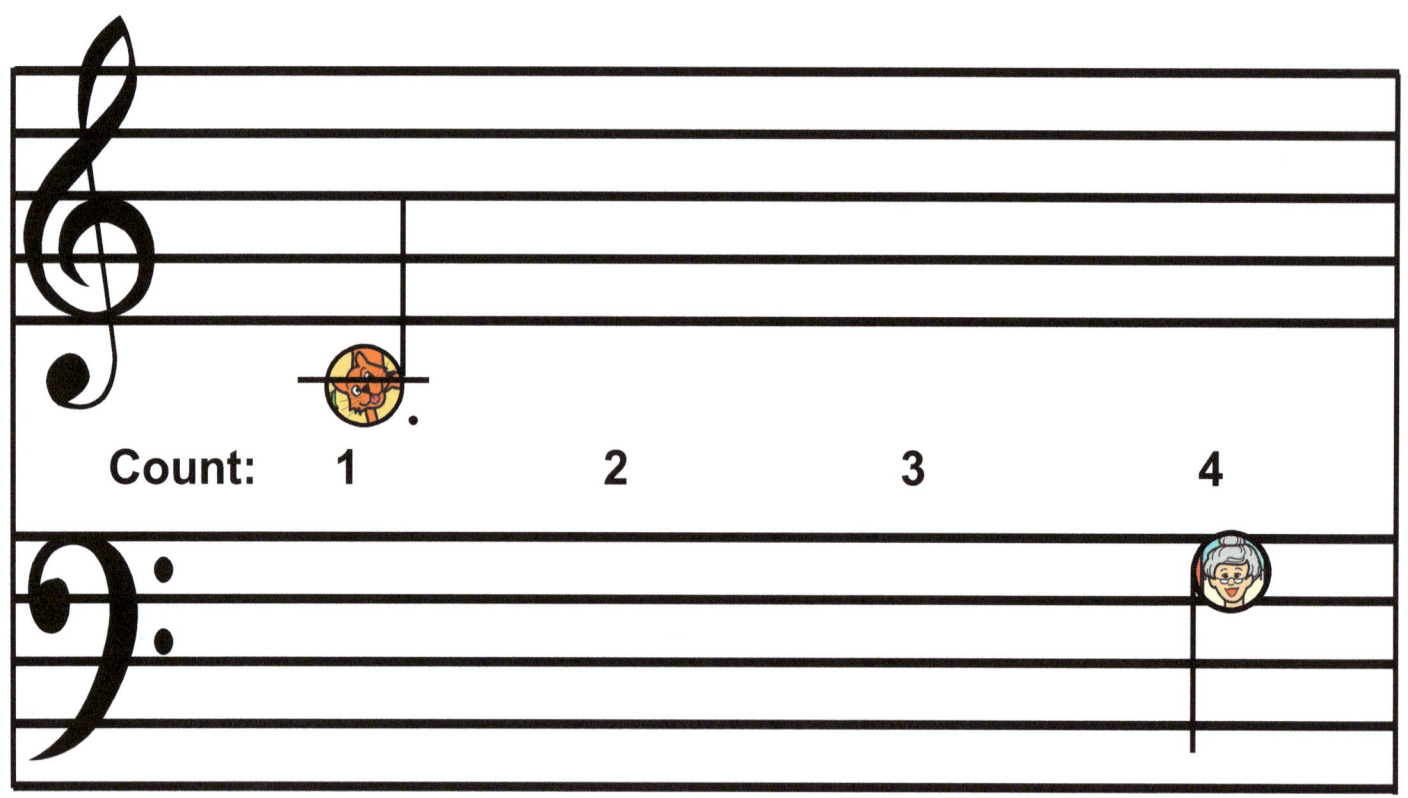

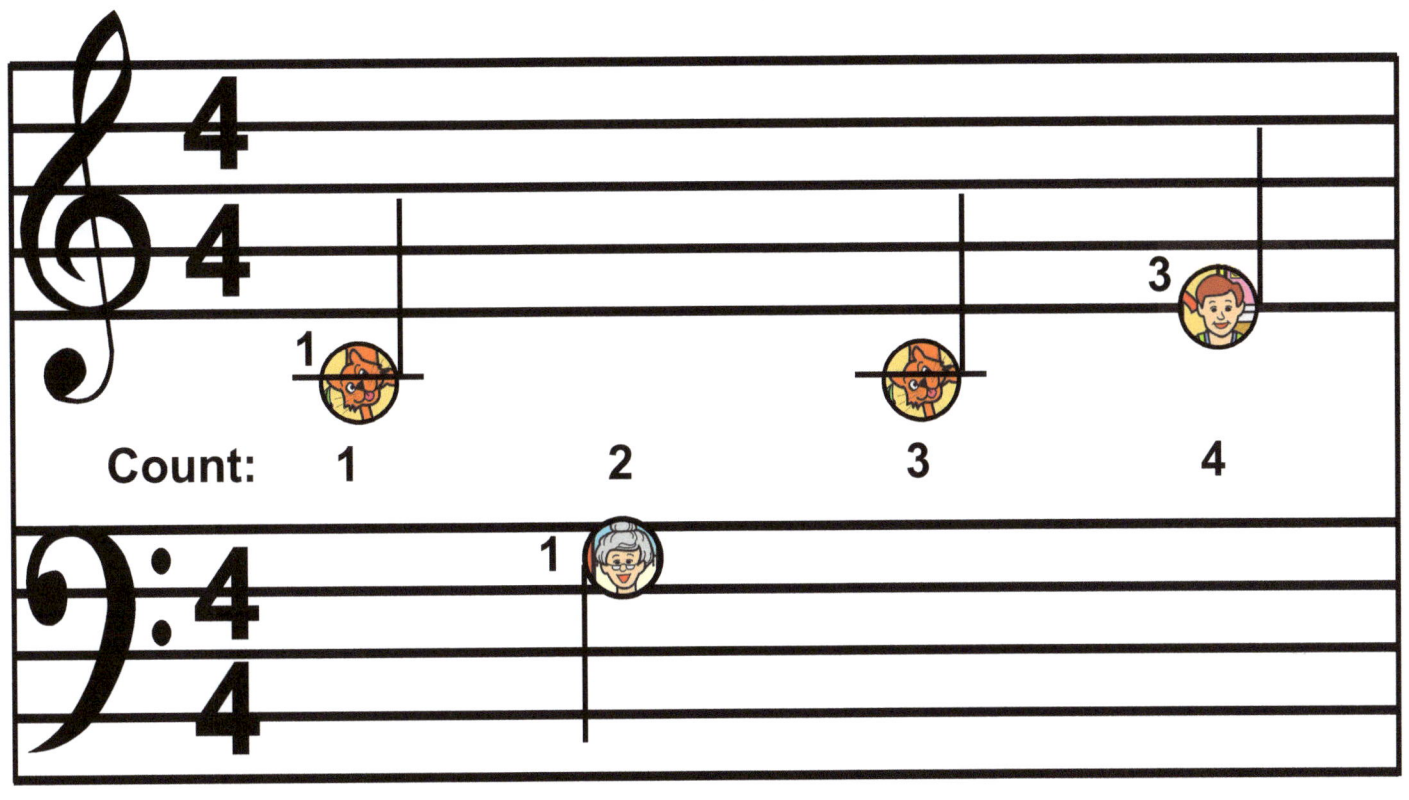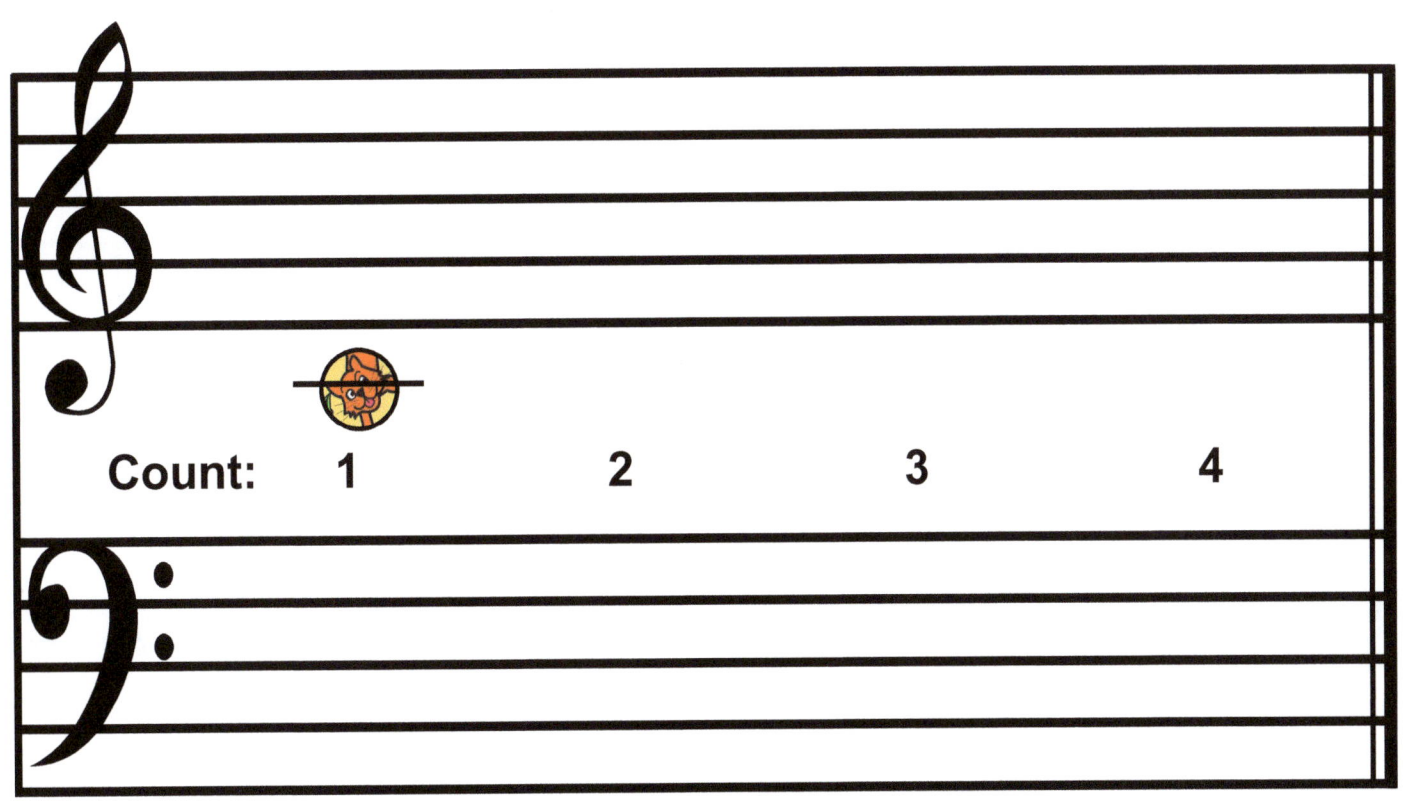

Jesus Christ Is Risen Today

Traditional

A more advanced version of this song is found in Picture Songs 4 More Songs of God and Country. Watch the fingering changes.

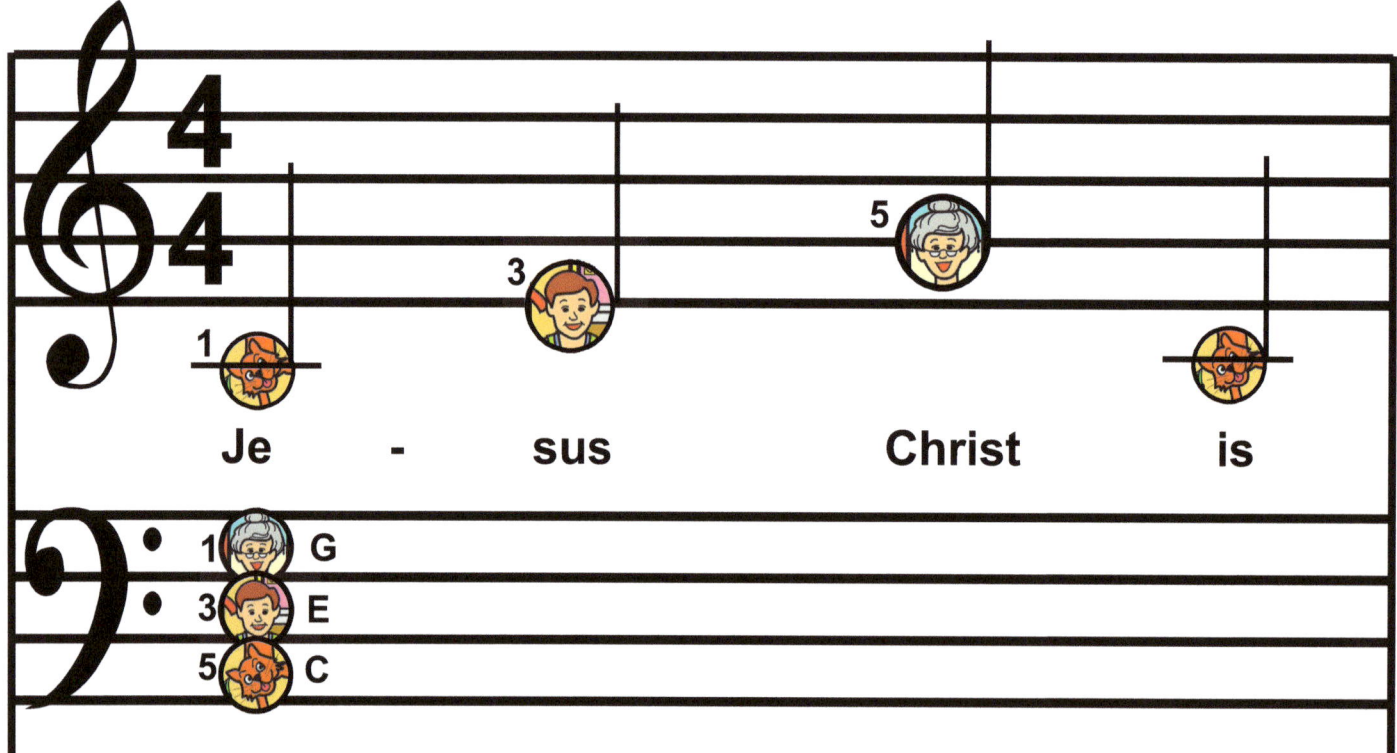

Je - sus　　　　Christ　　　is

Move finger 3 to F here.

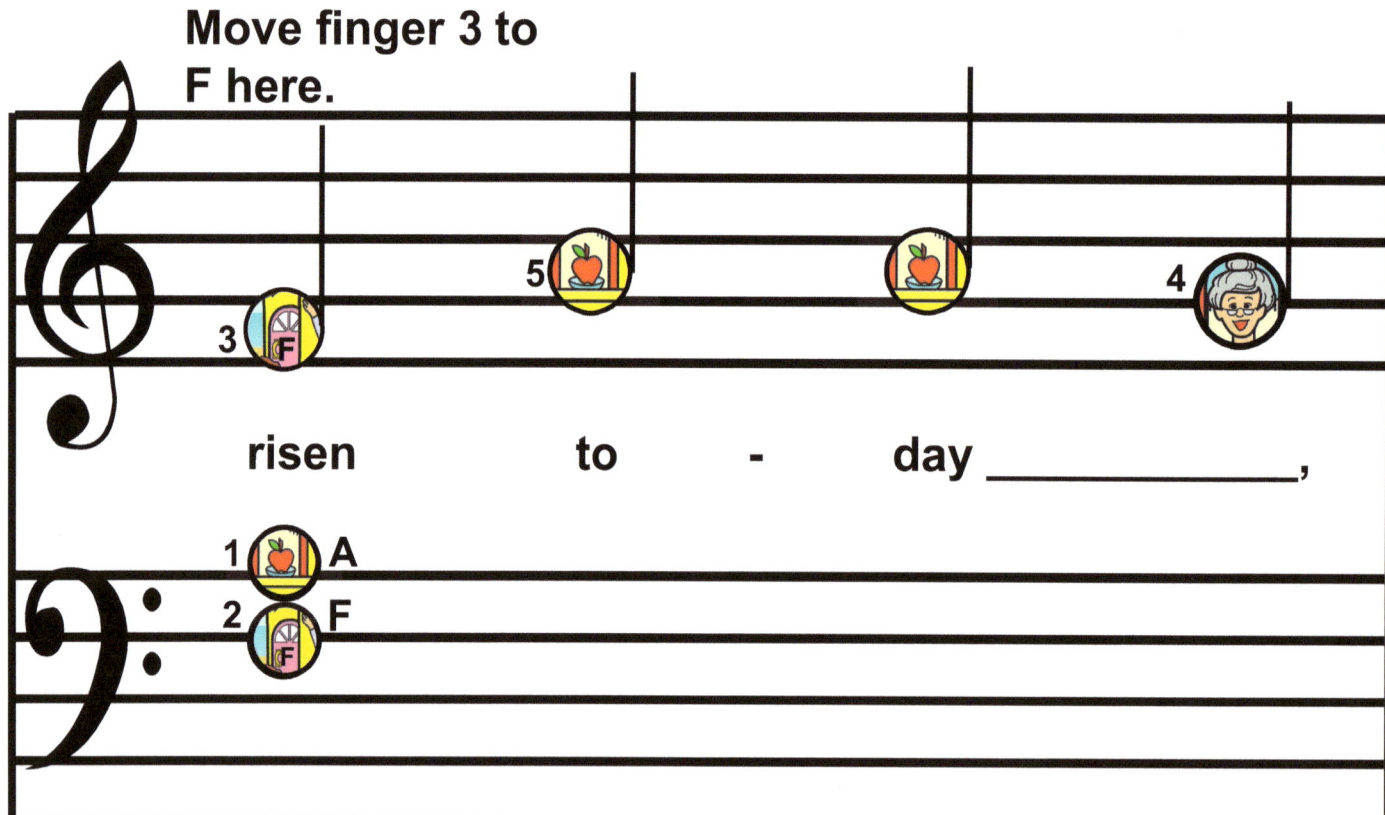

risen　　　to - day _____,

40

When notes are joined together with a bridge they are played a little faster.

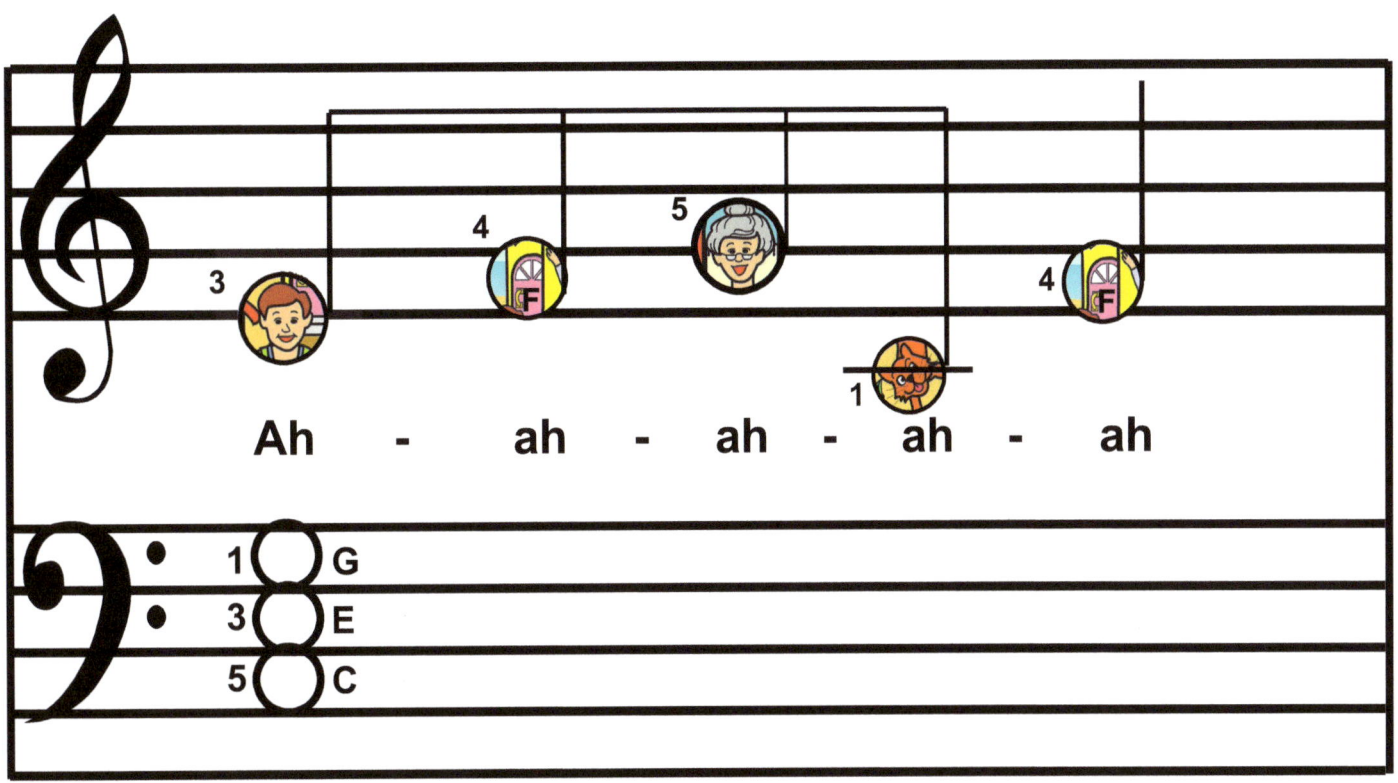

CLIMBING THE LADDER

These big lines are the ladder for climbing up and down the music pages. Climb up 8 steps on the ladder from middle C to your right. Now you are in the next neighborhood up on the music page and on the piano keyboard also. On your piano keyboard move your Cat C block from Middle C to the next neighborhood to your right for the next song in this book.

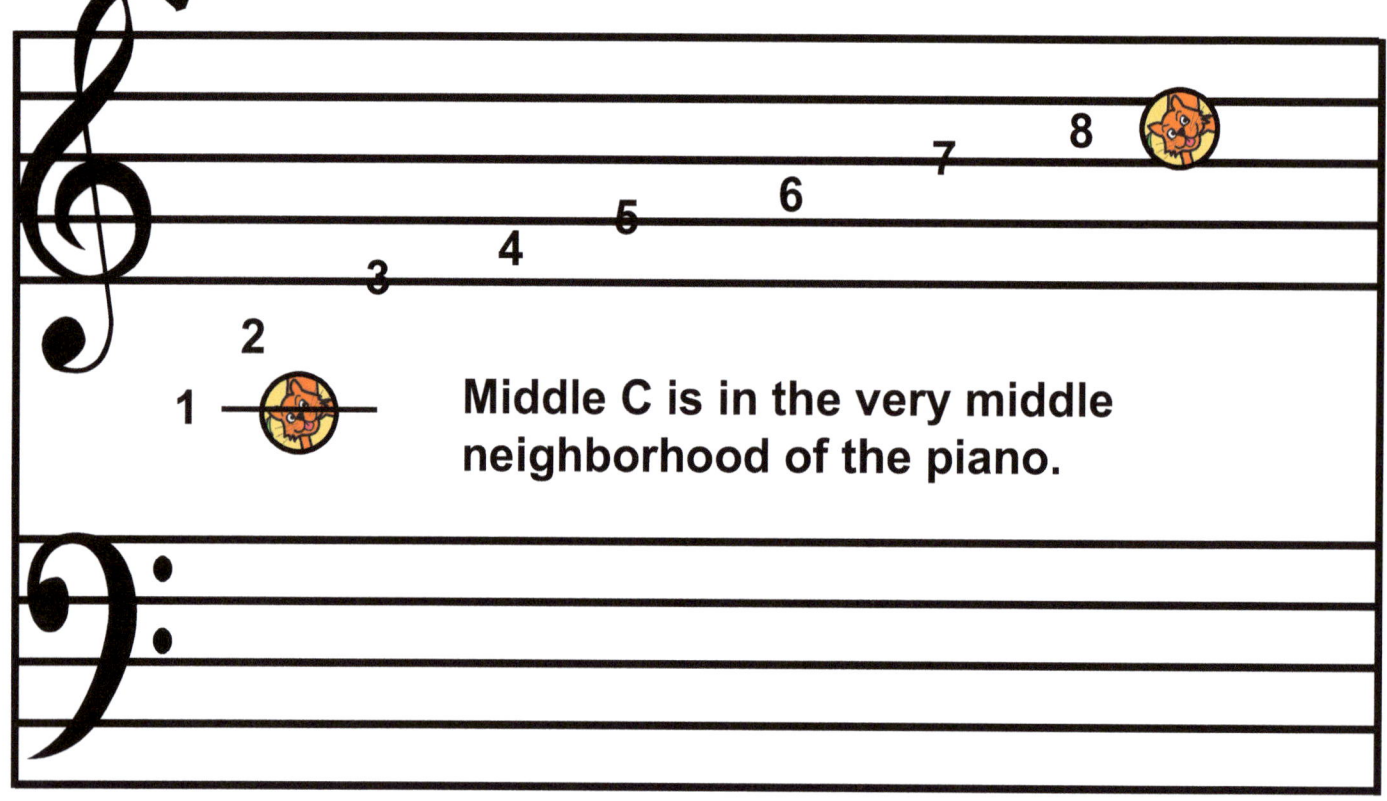

Middle C is in the very middle neighborhood of the piano.

Up the ladder to your right to the high sounding notes on your music pages. High notes sound like birds chirping high in the trees.

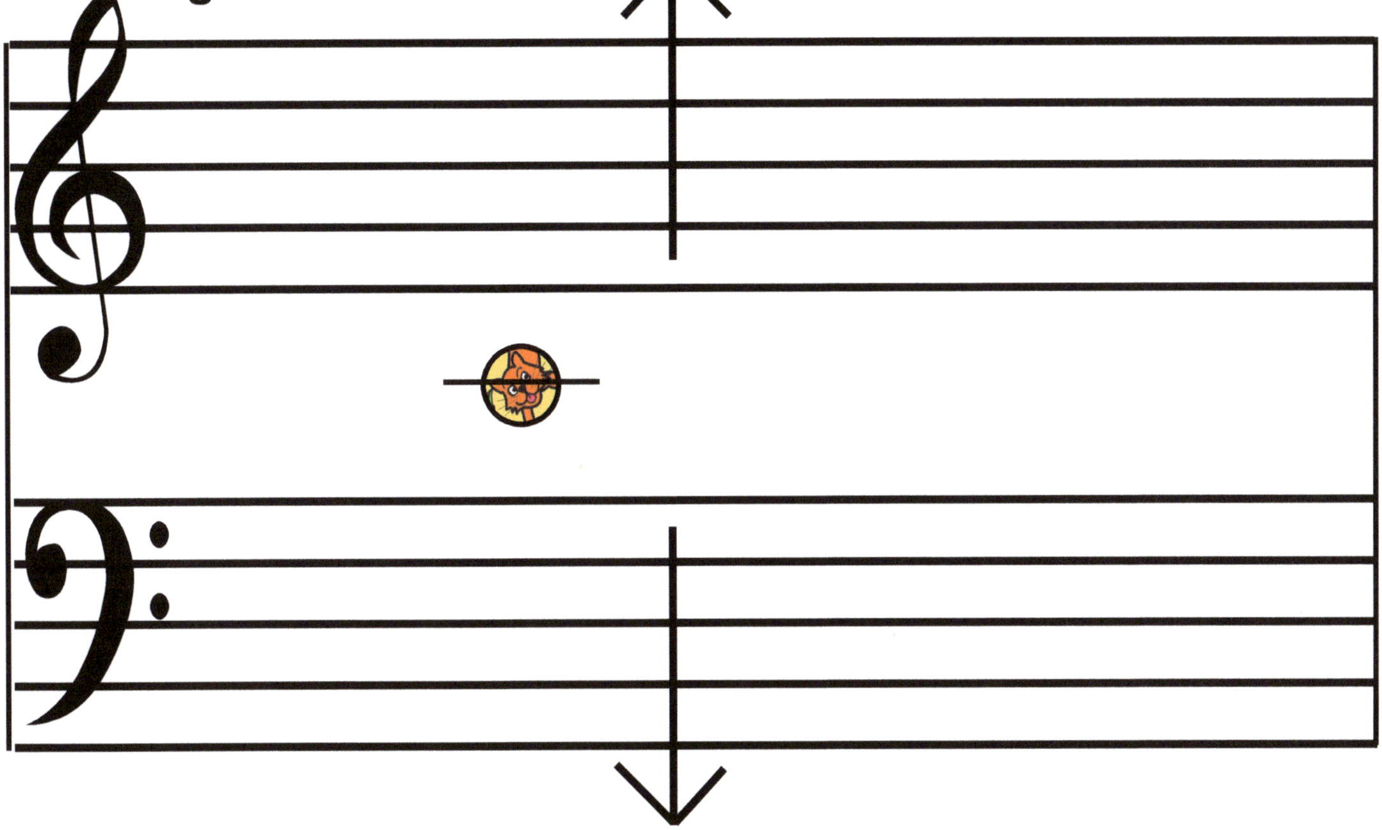

Down the ladder to your left to the low sounding notes on your music pages. Low notes sound like an elephant stomping on the ground.

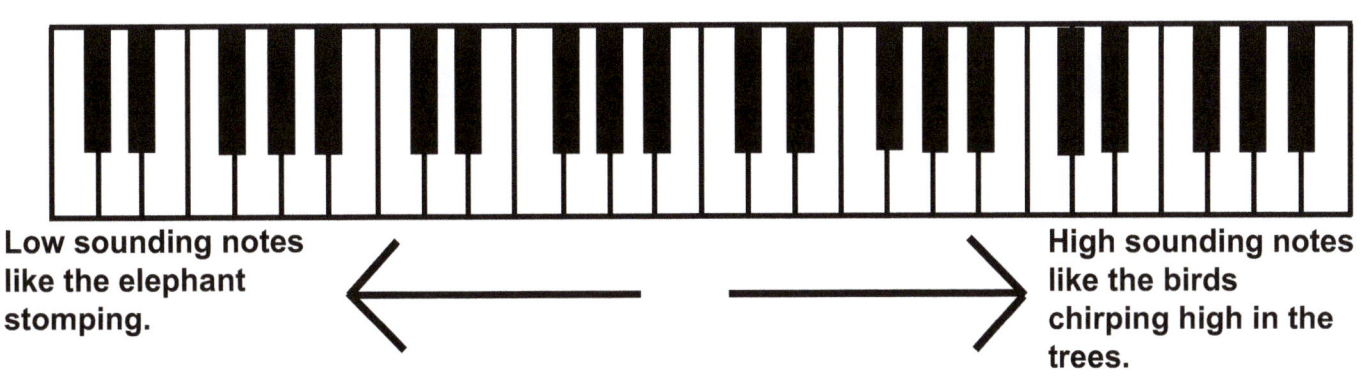

Low sounding notes like the elephant stomping.

High sounding notes like the birds chirping high in the trees.

DOWN   **UP**

HALLELUJAH CHORUS

J. F. Handel

Put your Cat C block in the neighborhood 8 notes to the right of middle C for your right hand. Be sure to watch the fingering numbers and change them when you need to.

Write in the names of the notes inside their circles. Or you can tell your parents what note it is and have them write in the note.

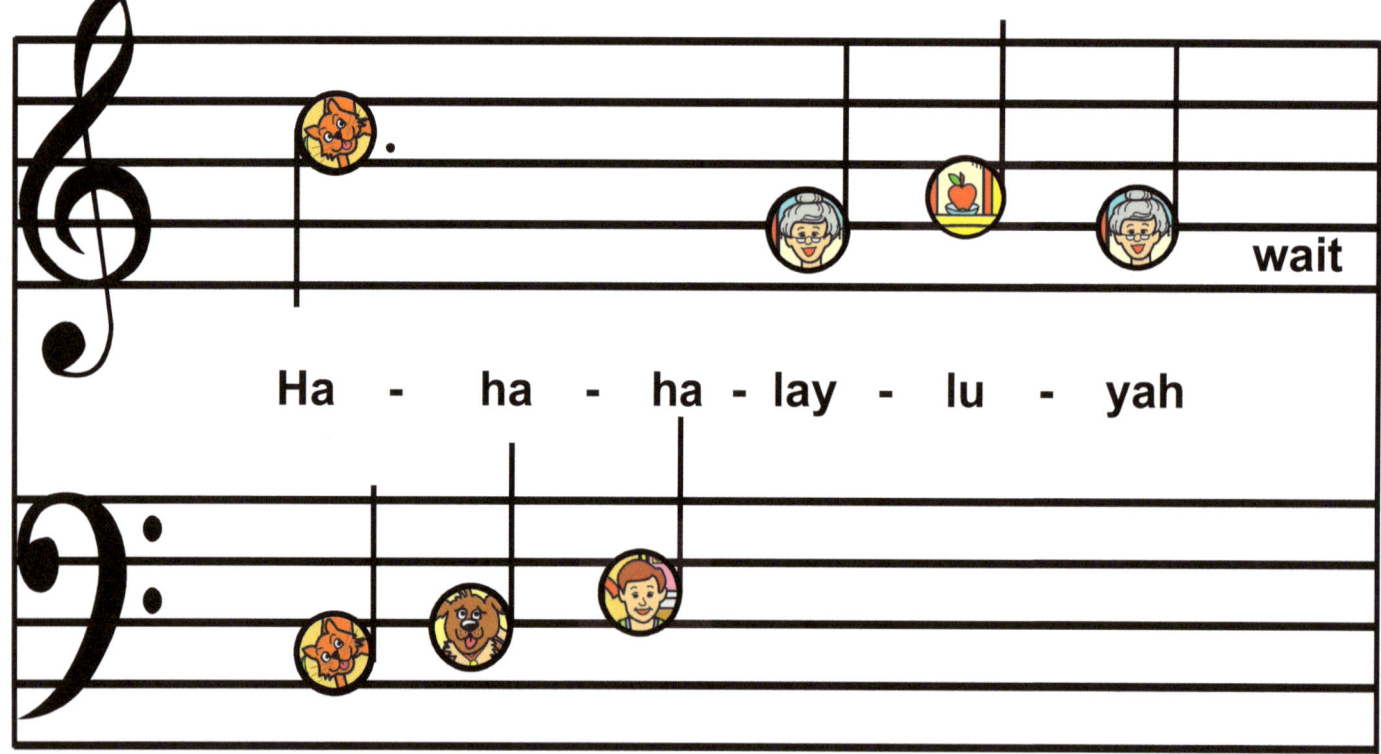

Write in the names of the notes inside their circles.   Or you can tell your parents what note it is and have them write in the note.

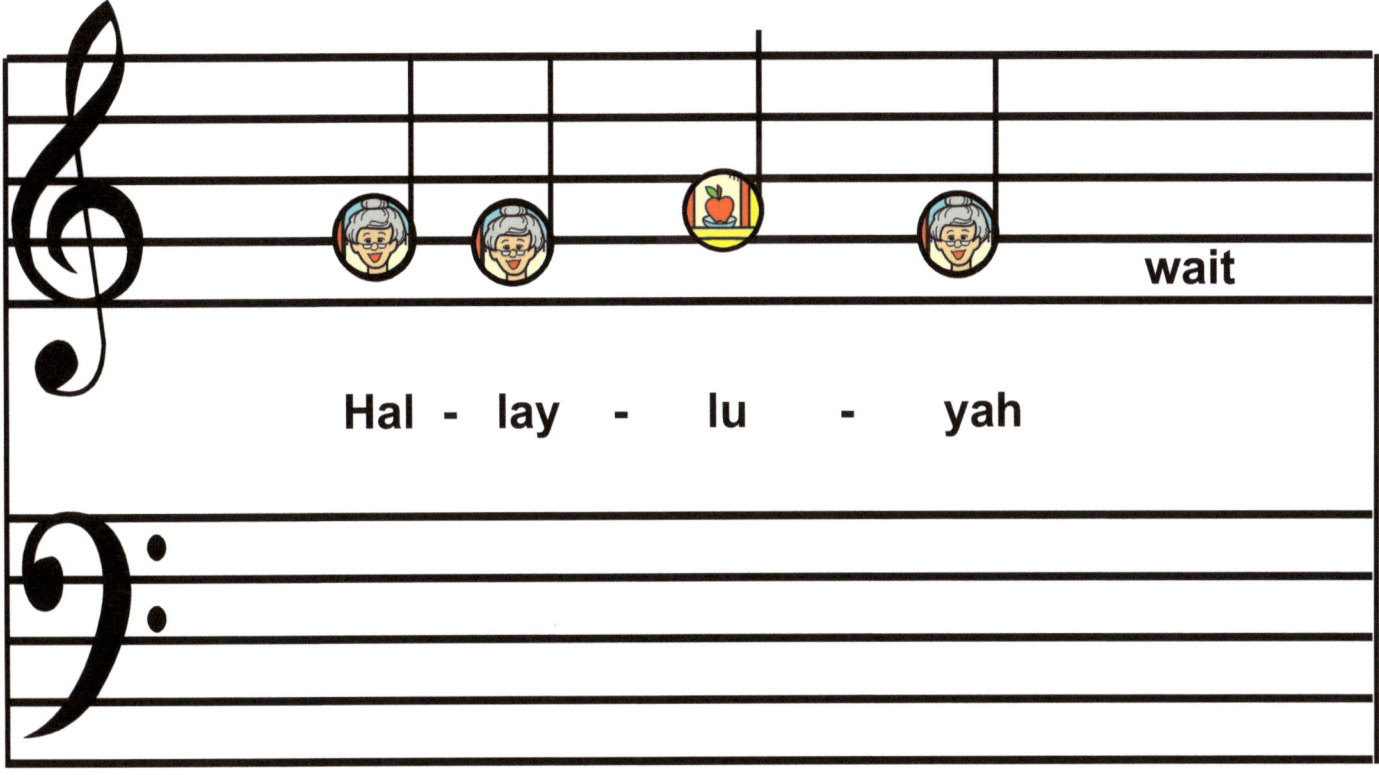

45

Change your right 4th finger to Grandma G.

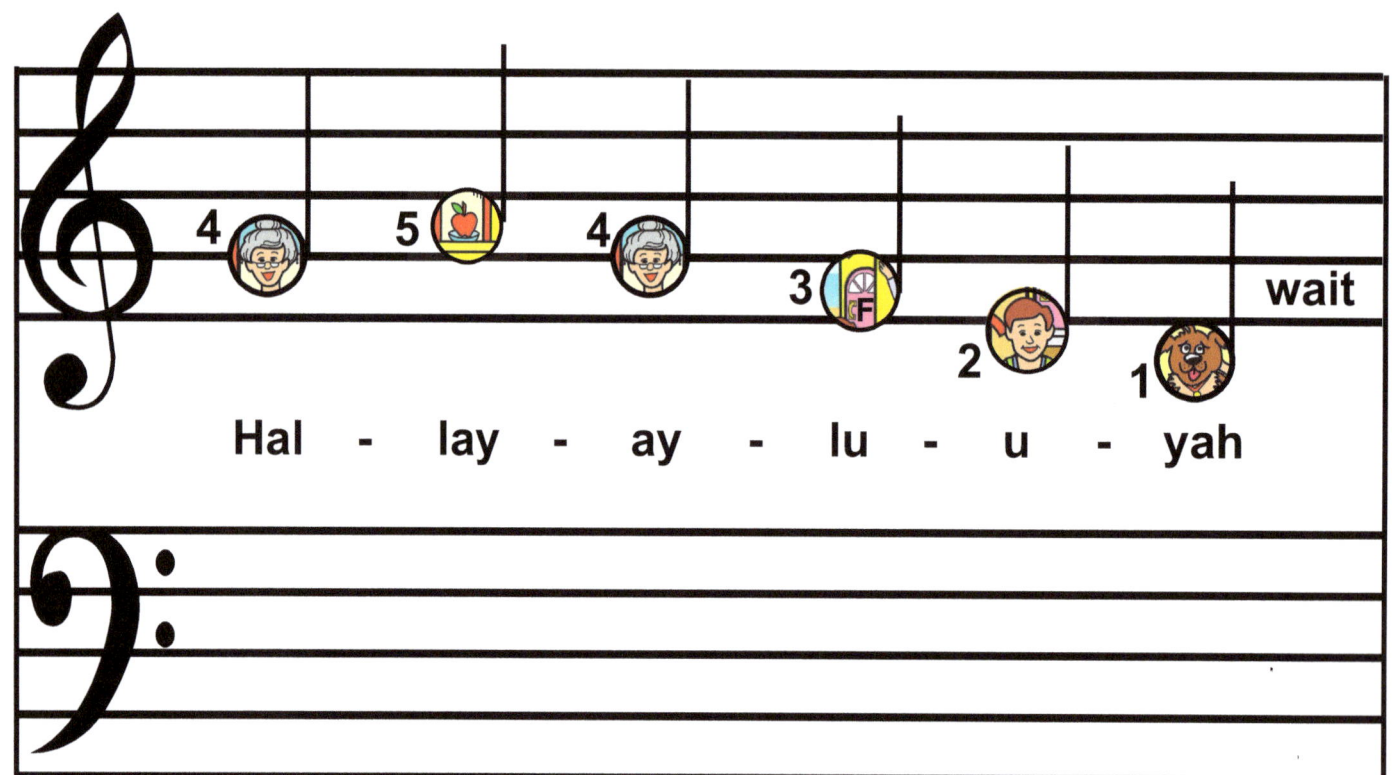

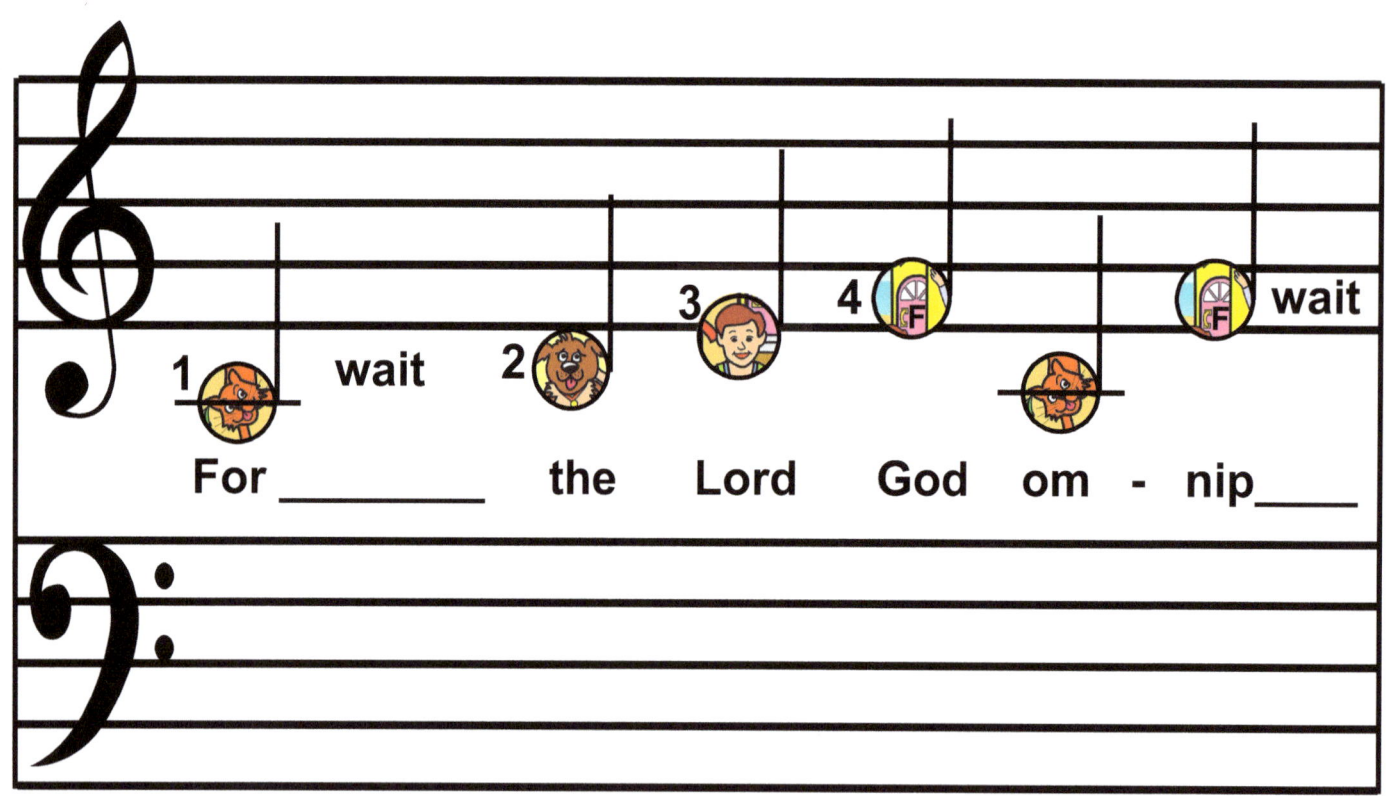

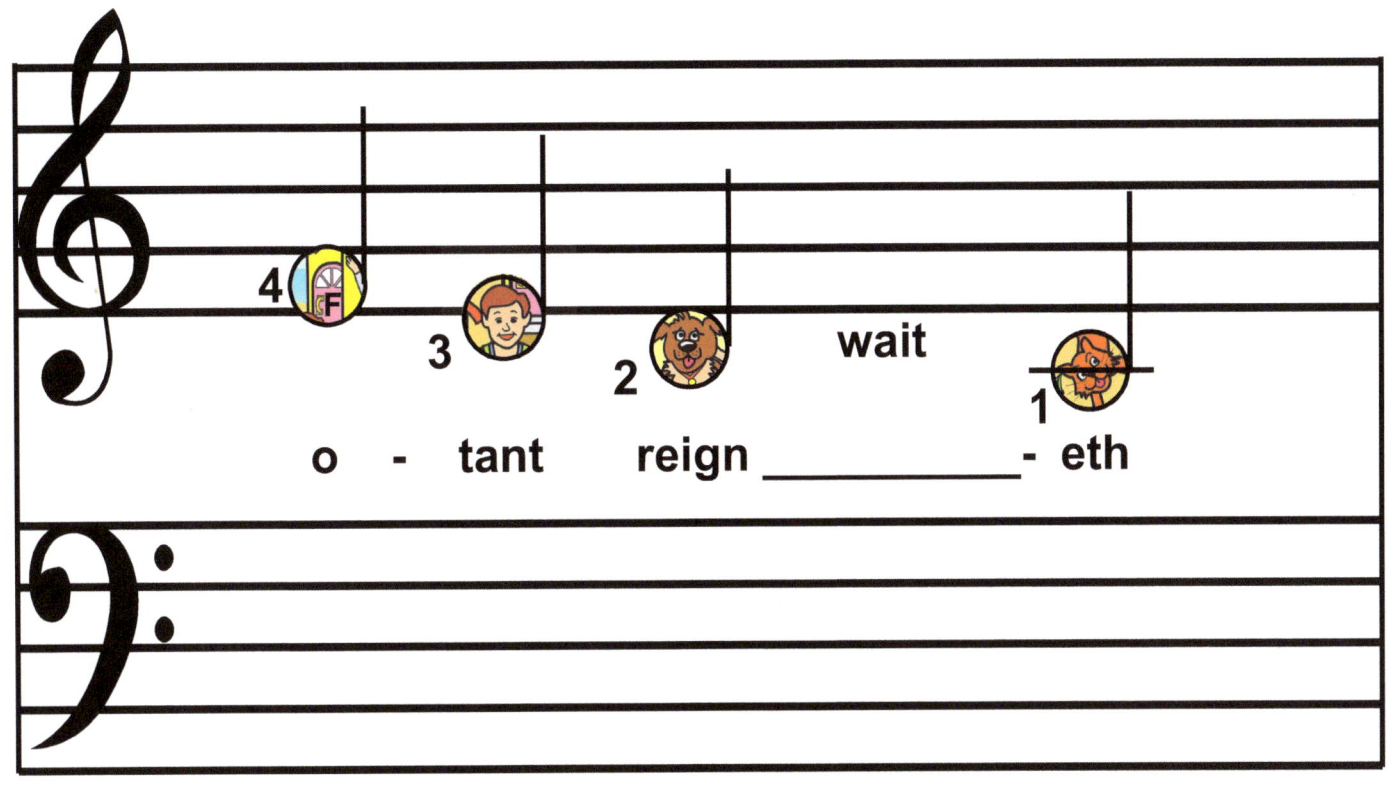
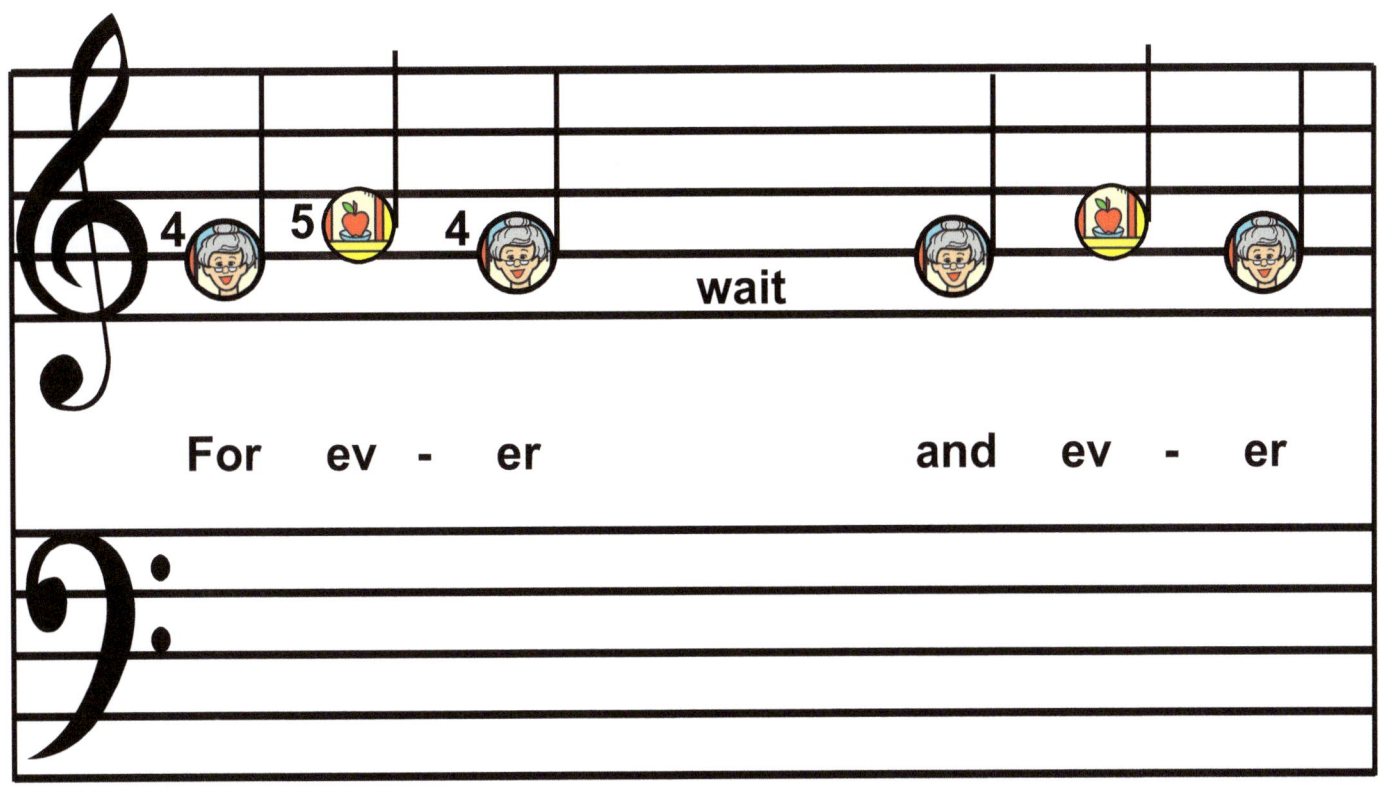

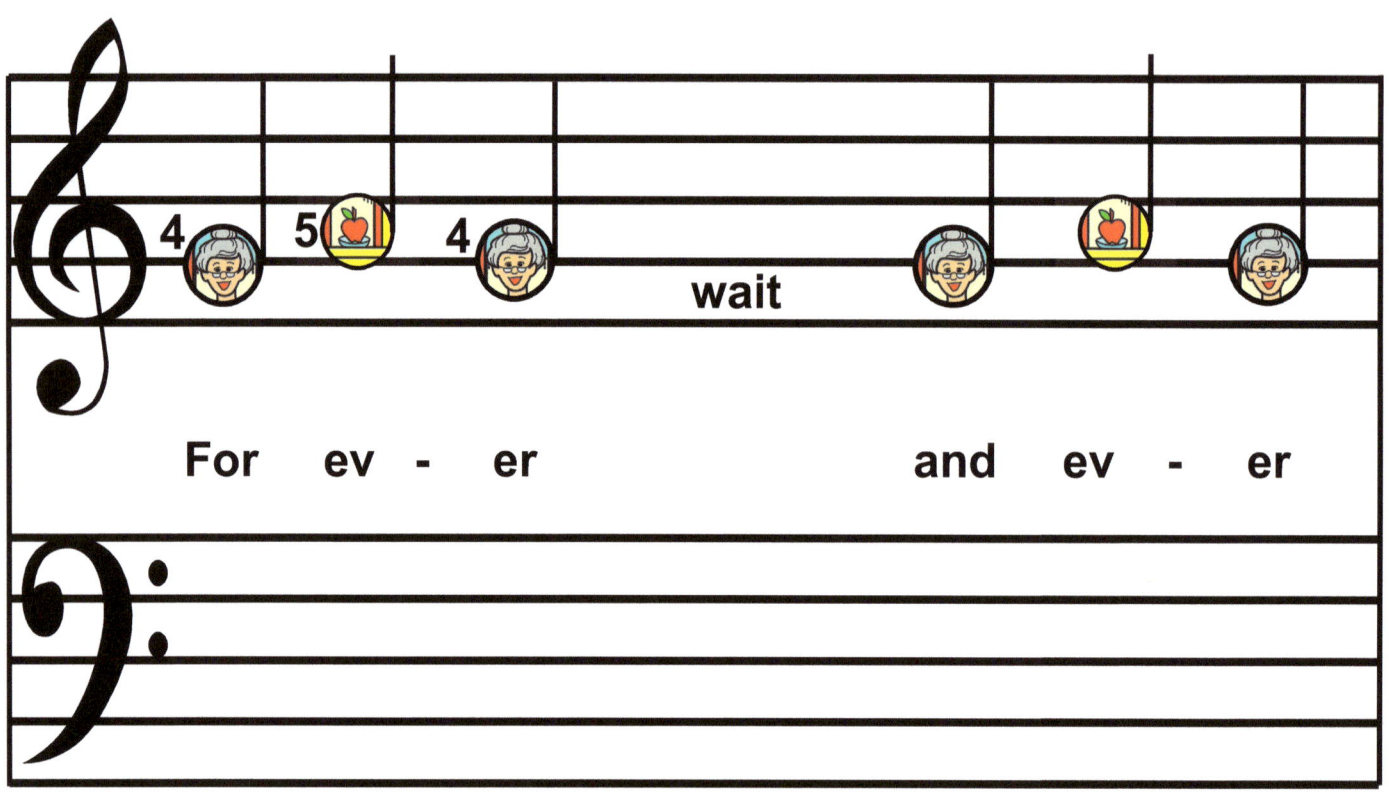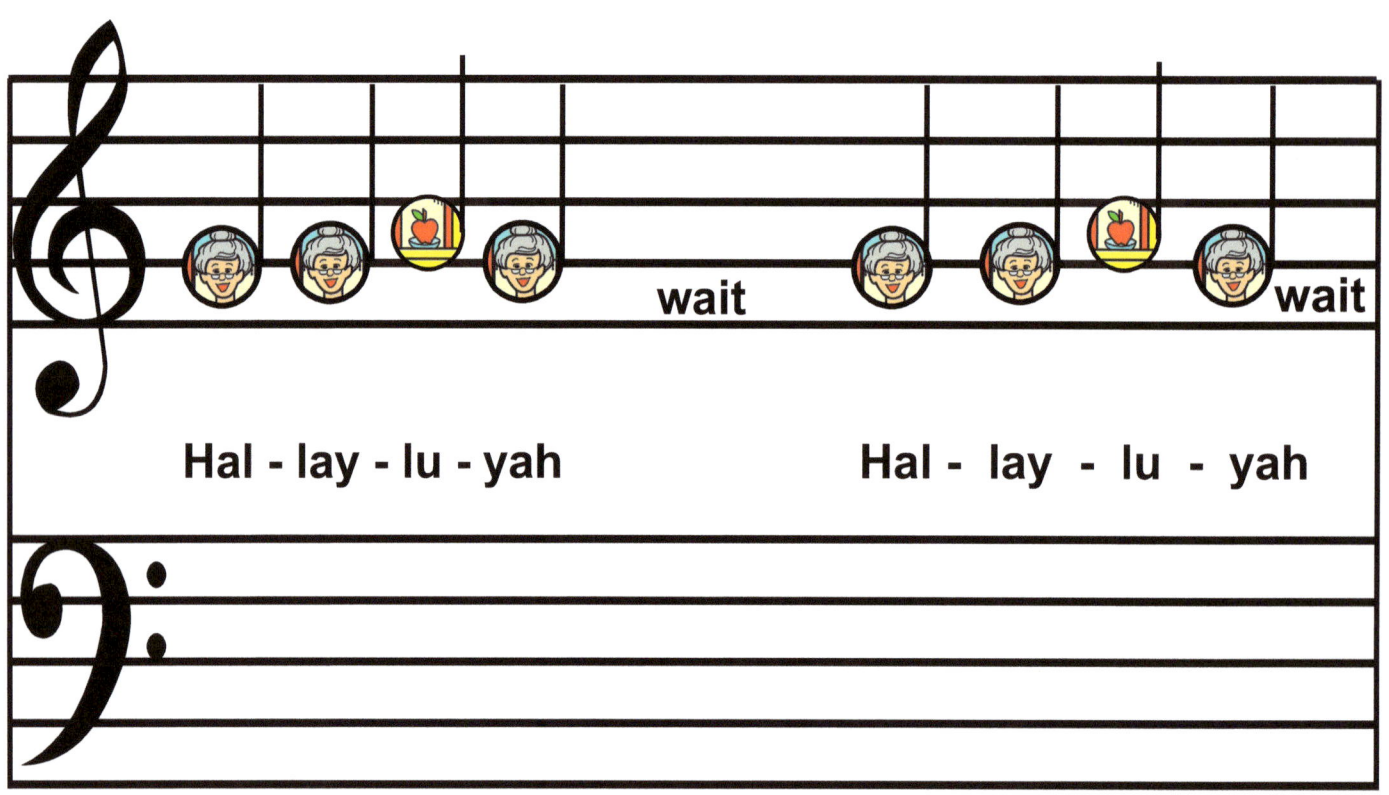

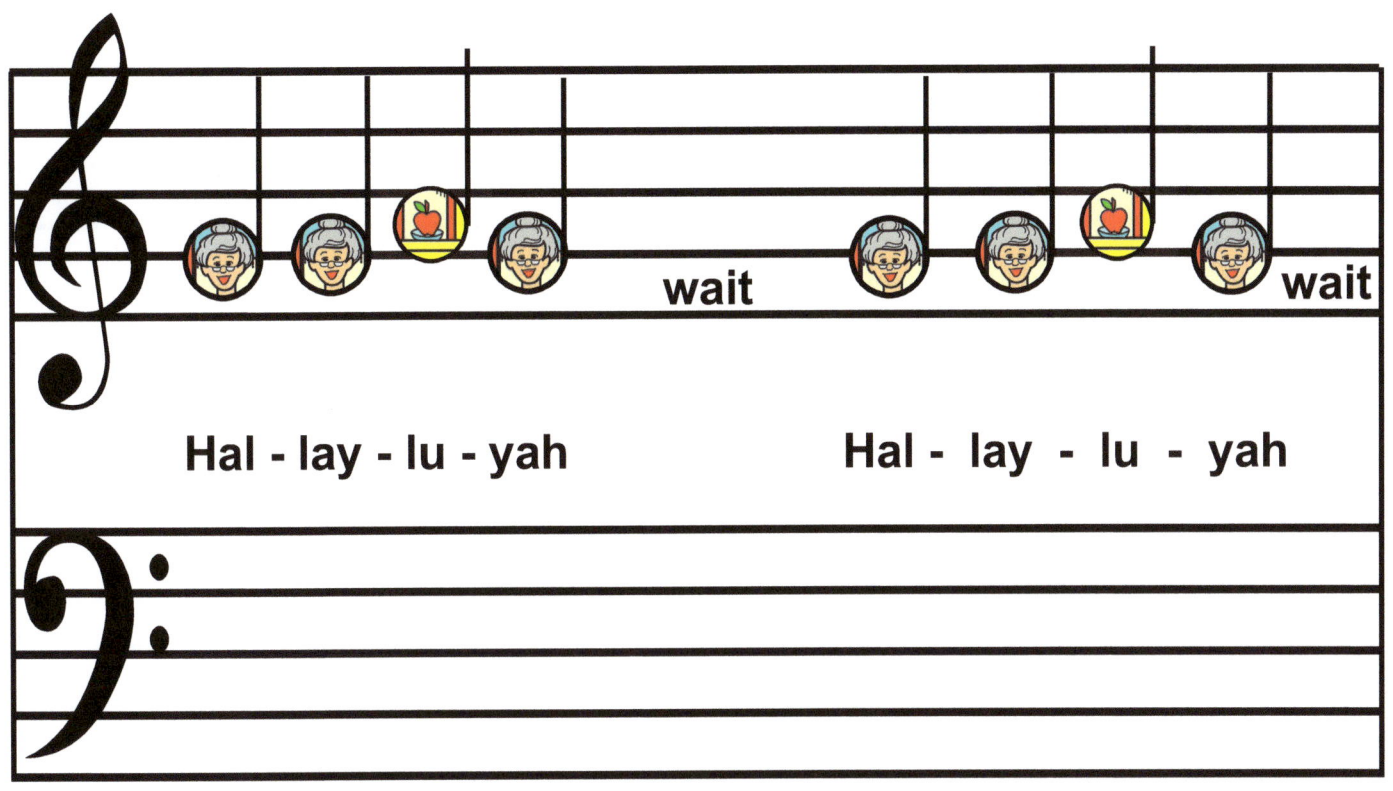
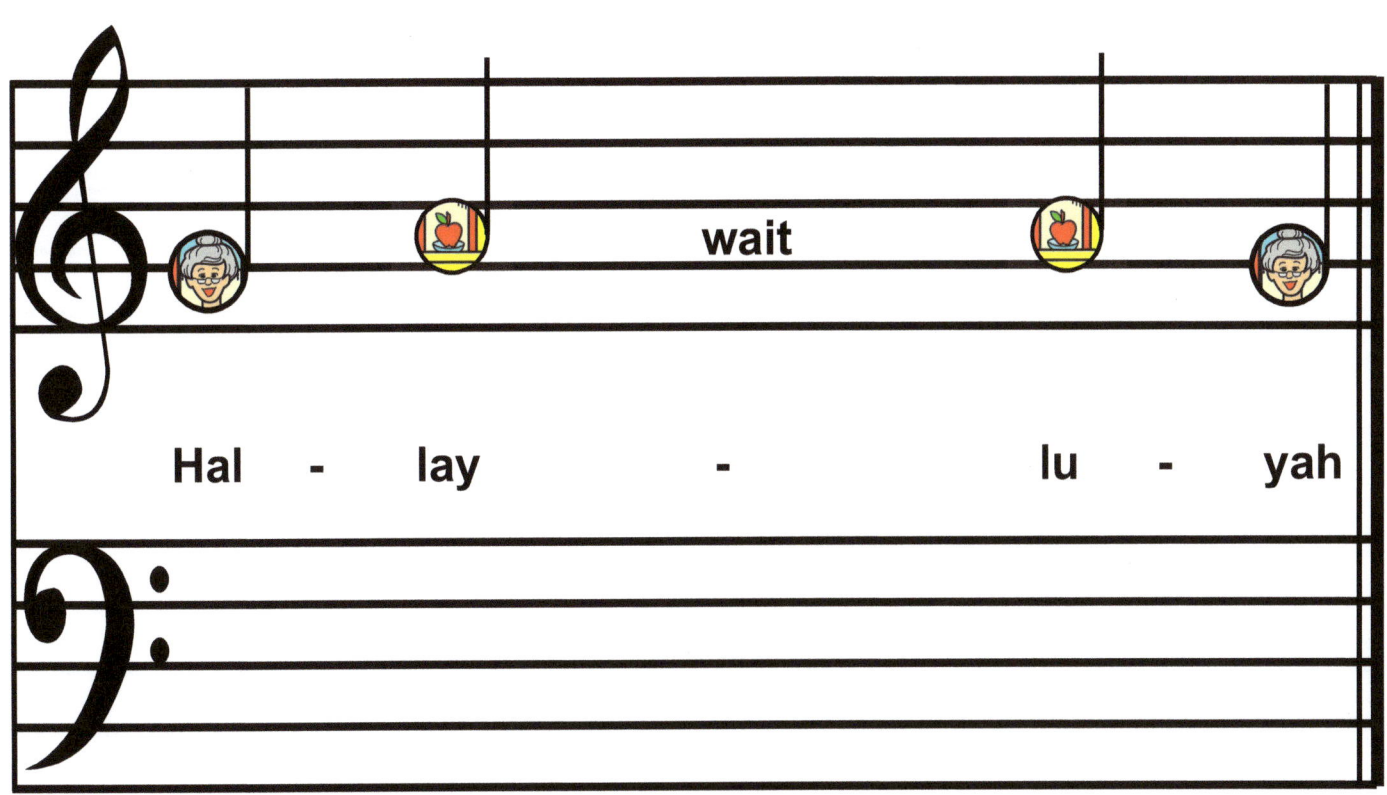

JESUS LOVES ME

Hand position: place both first fingers (thumbs) on middle C to share..

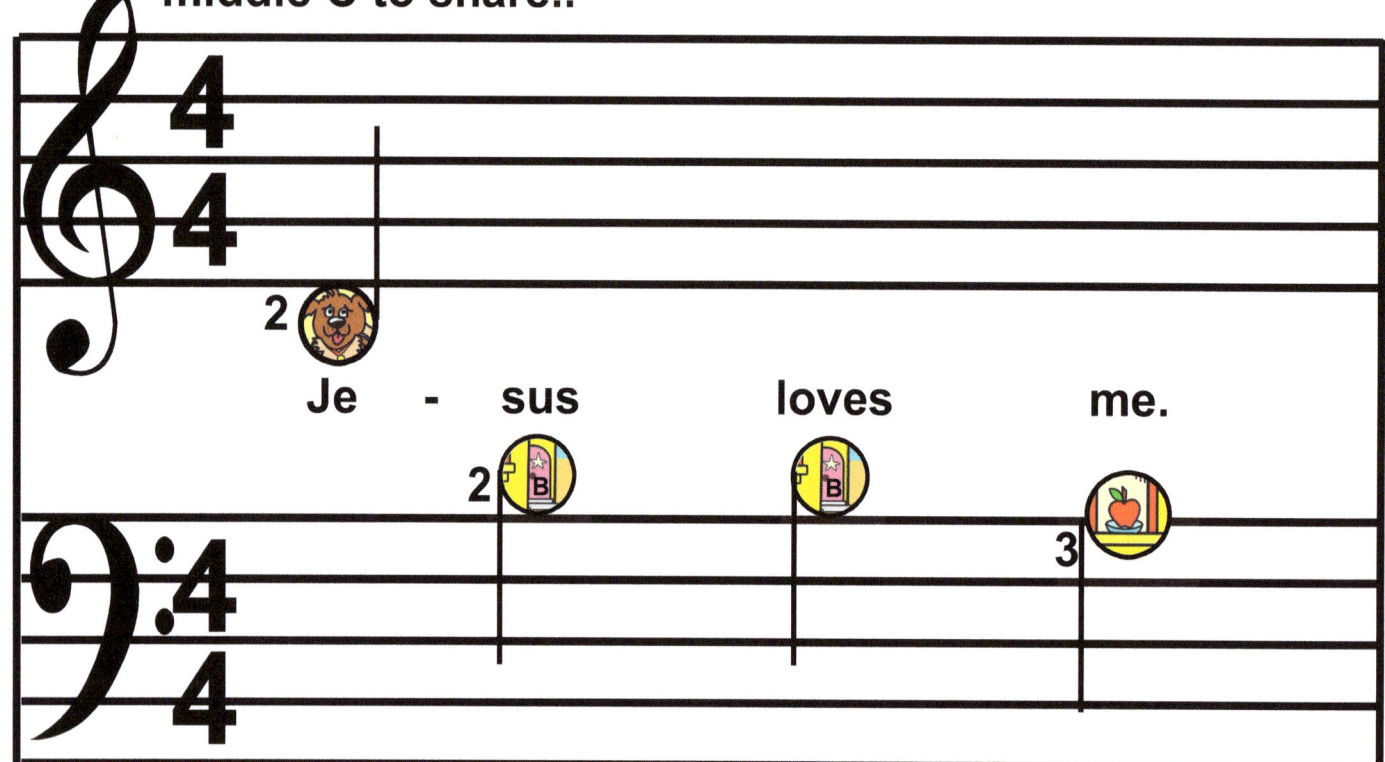

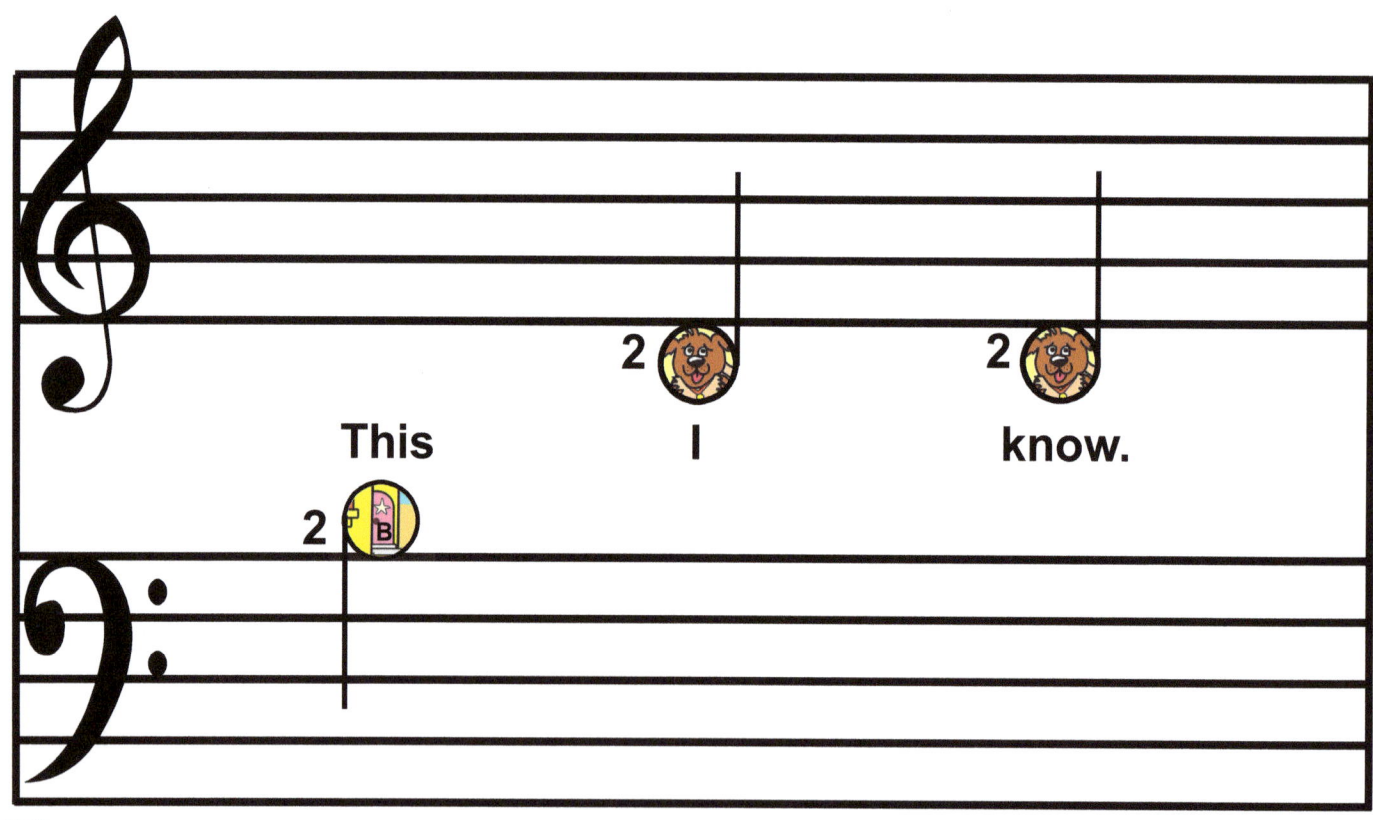

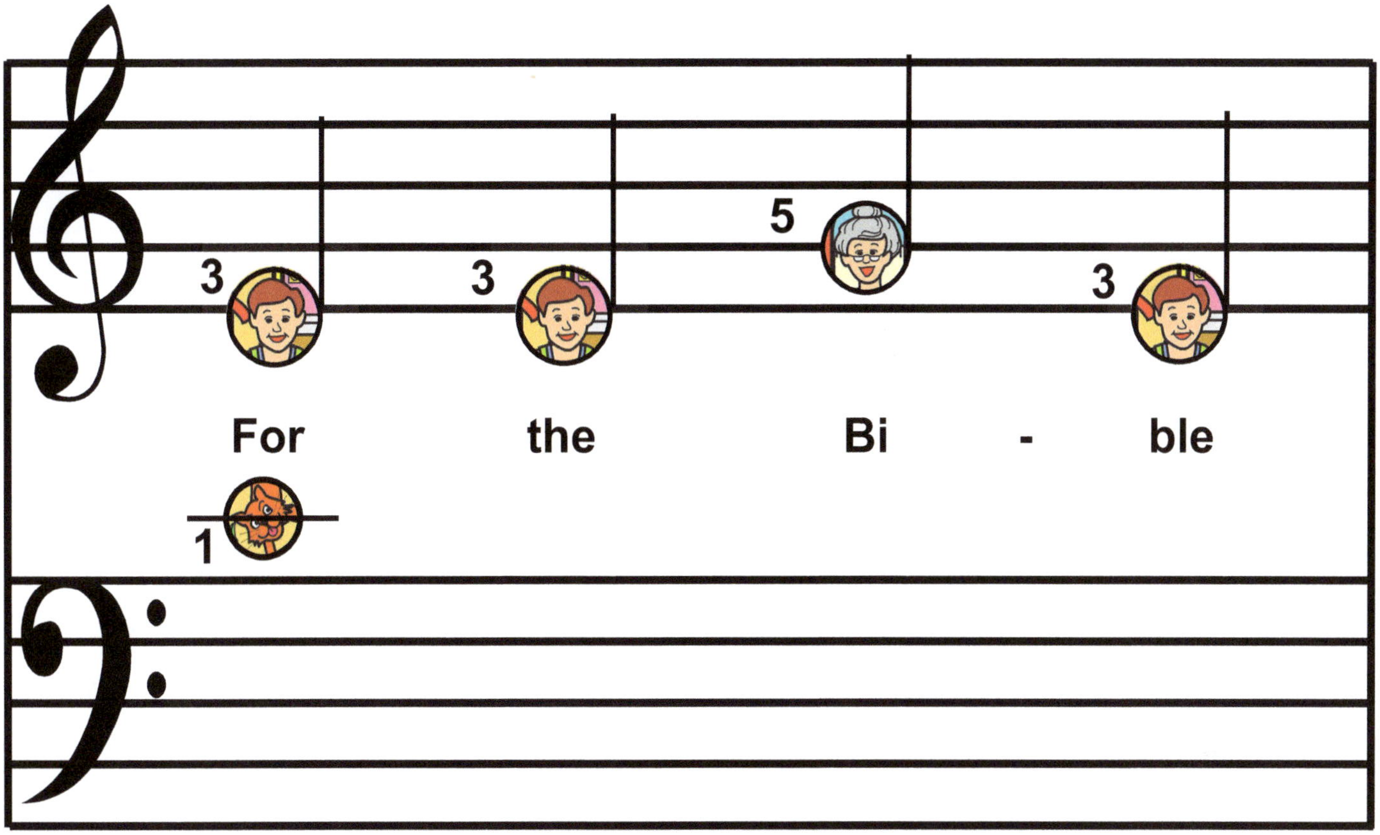
3 3 5 3
For the Bi - ble
1

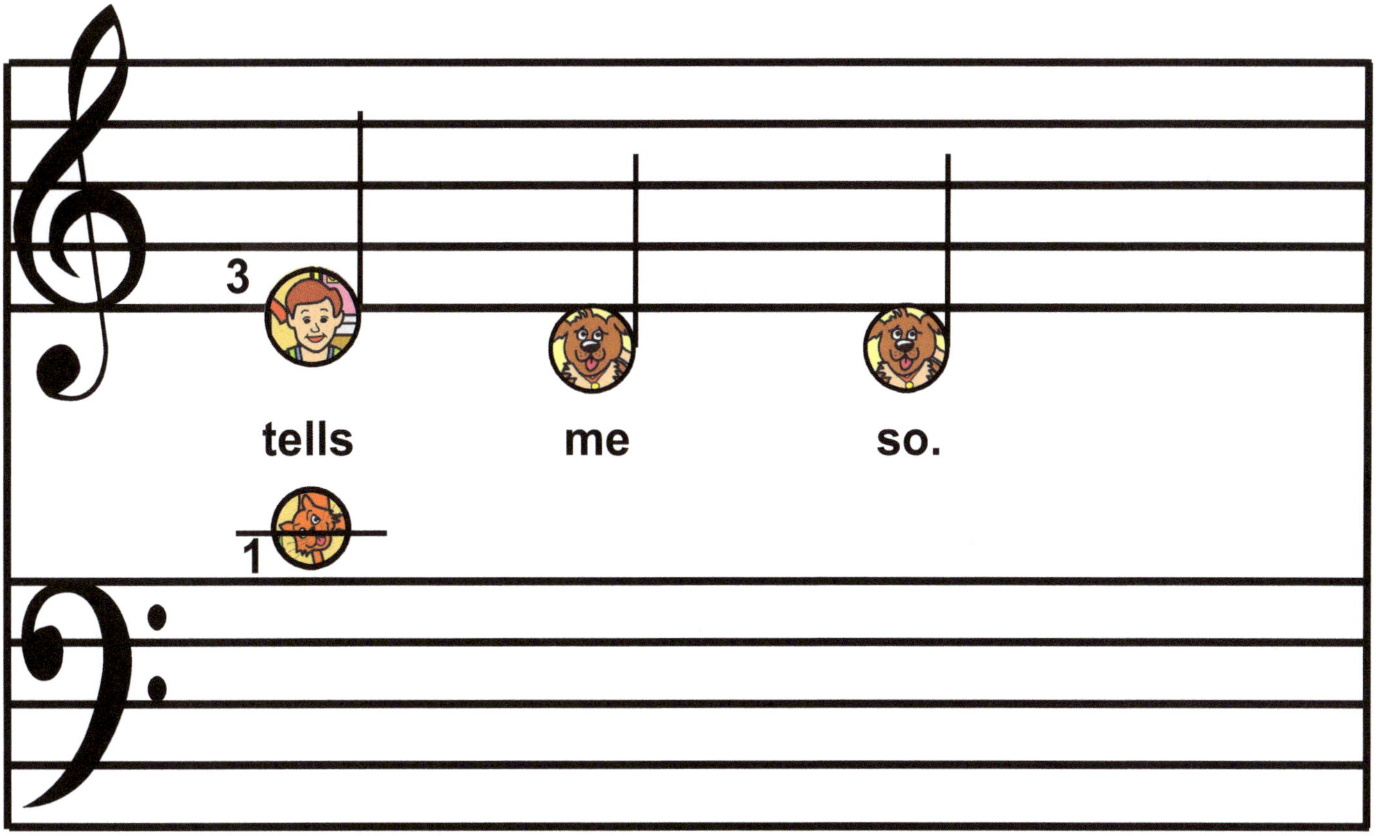
3
tells me so.
1

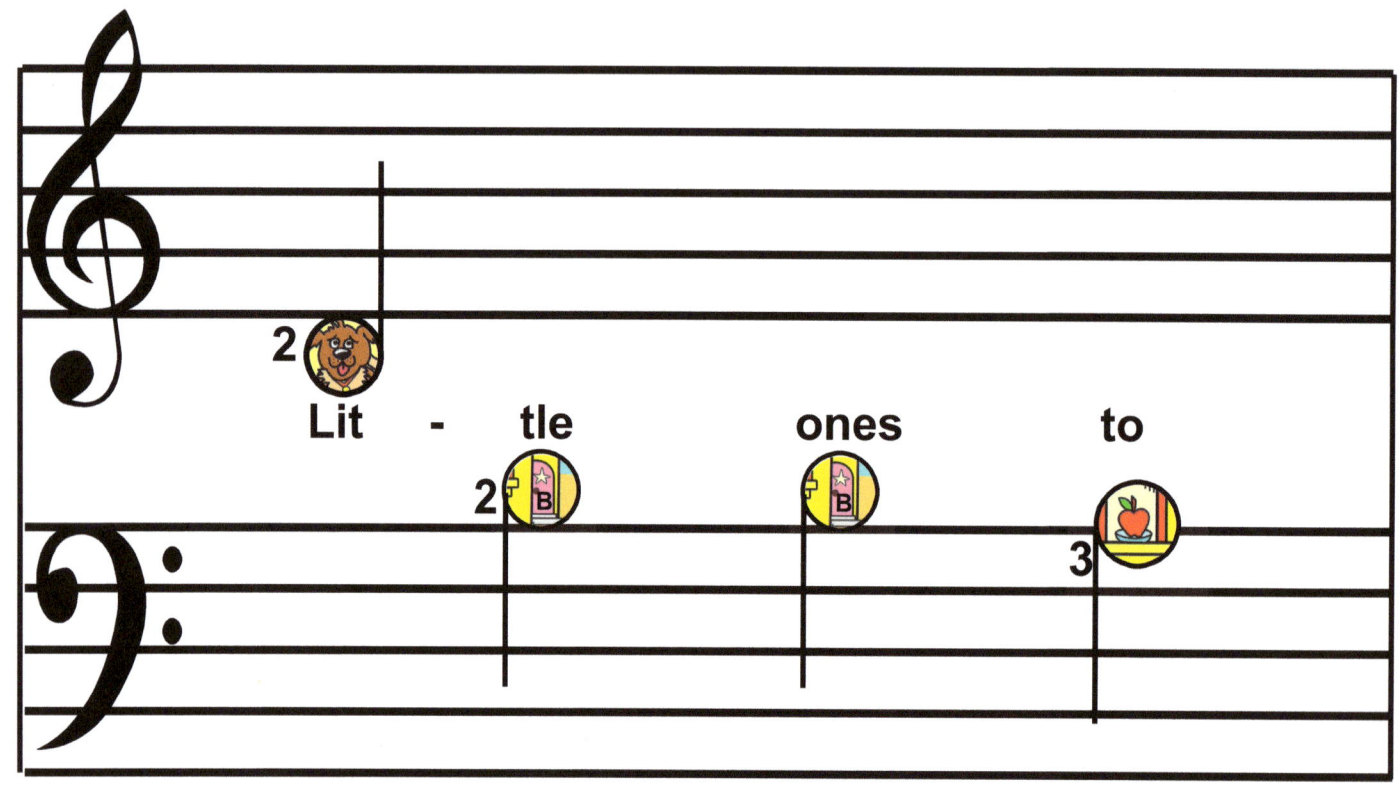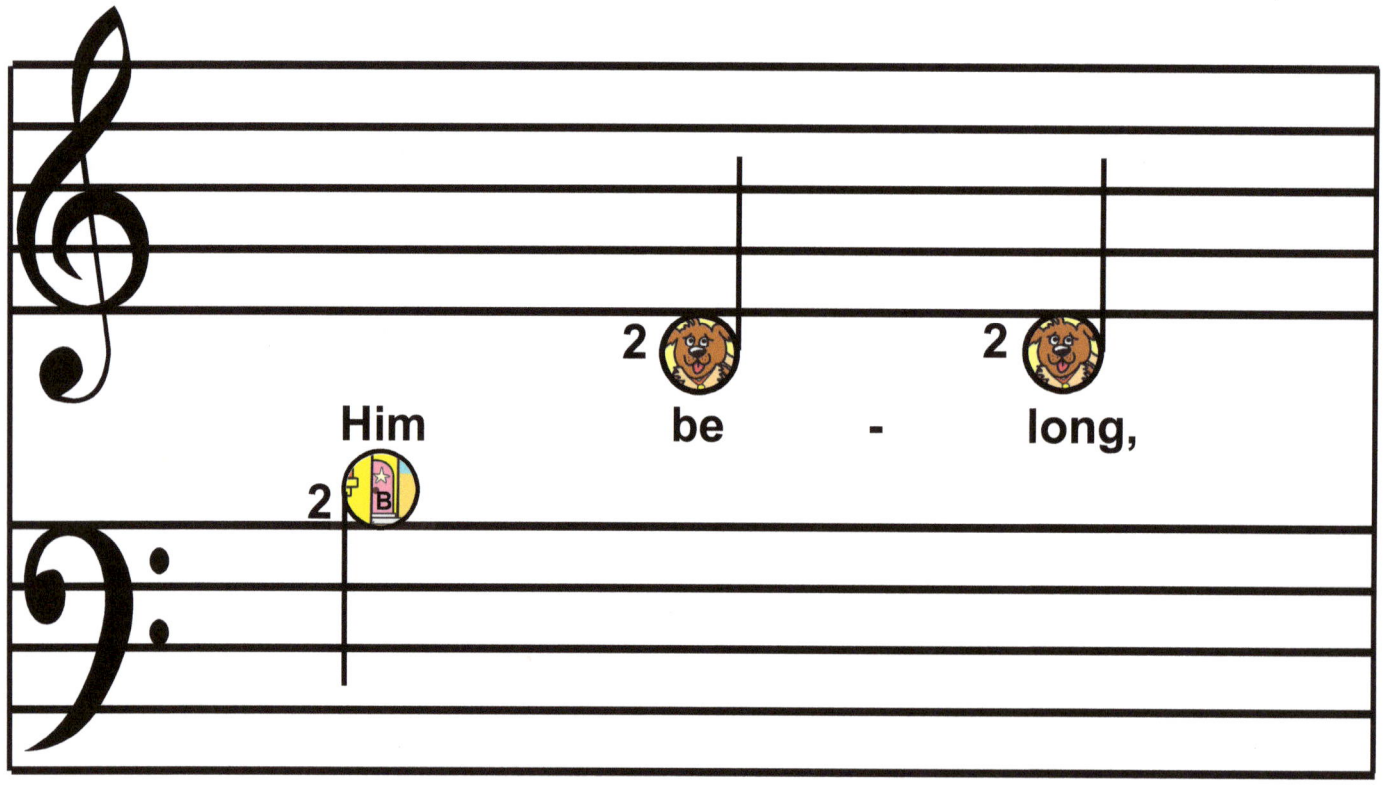

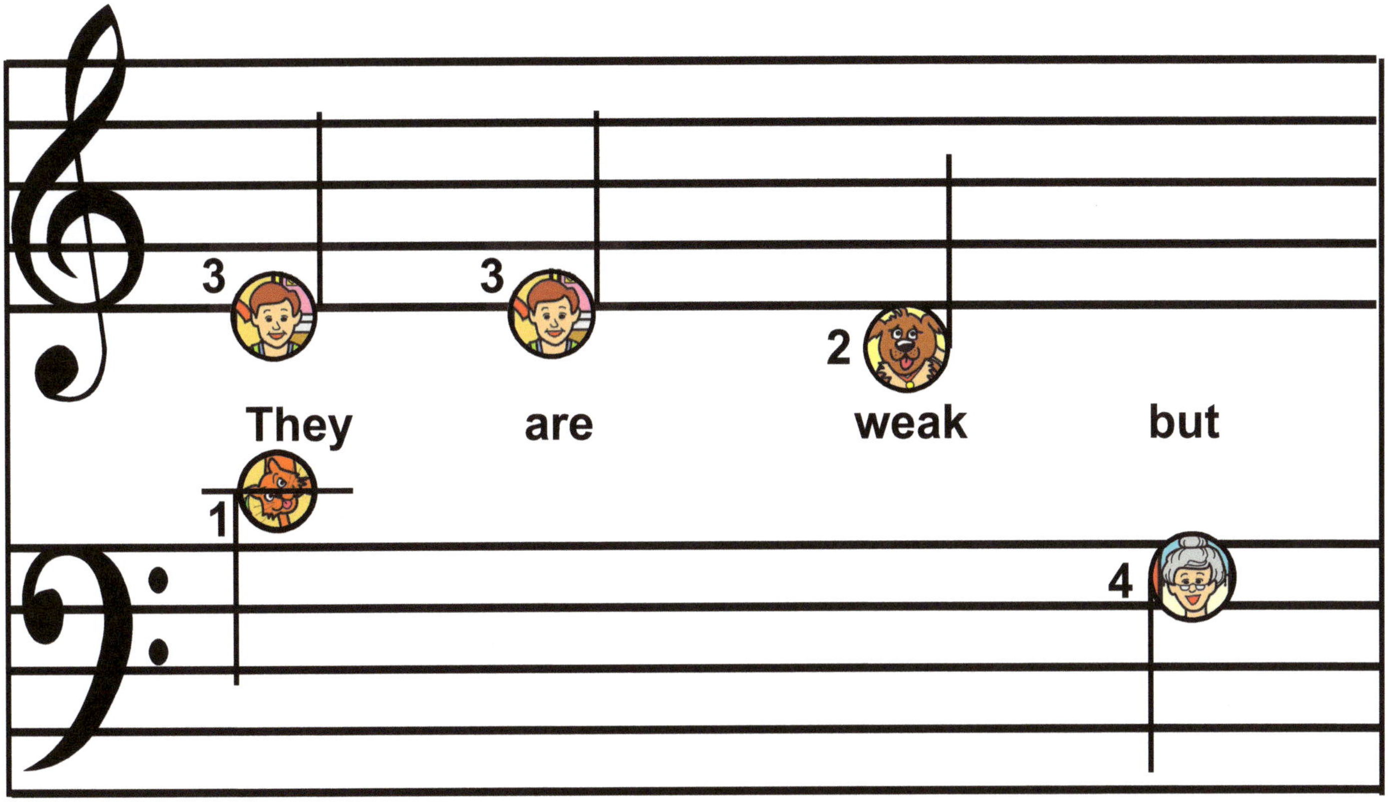

They are weak but 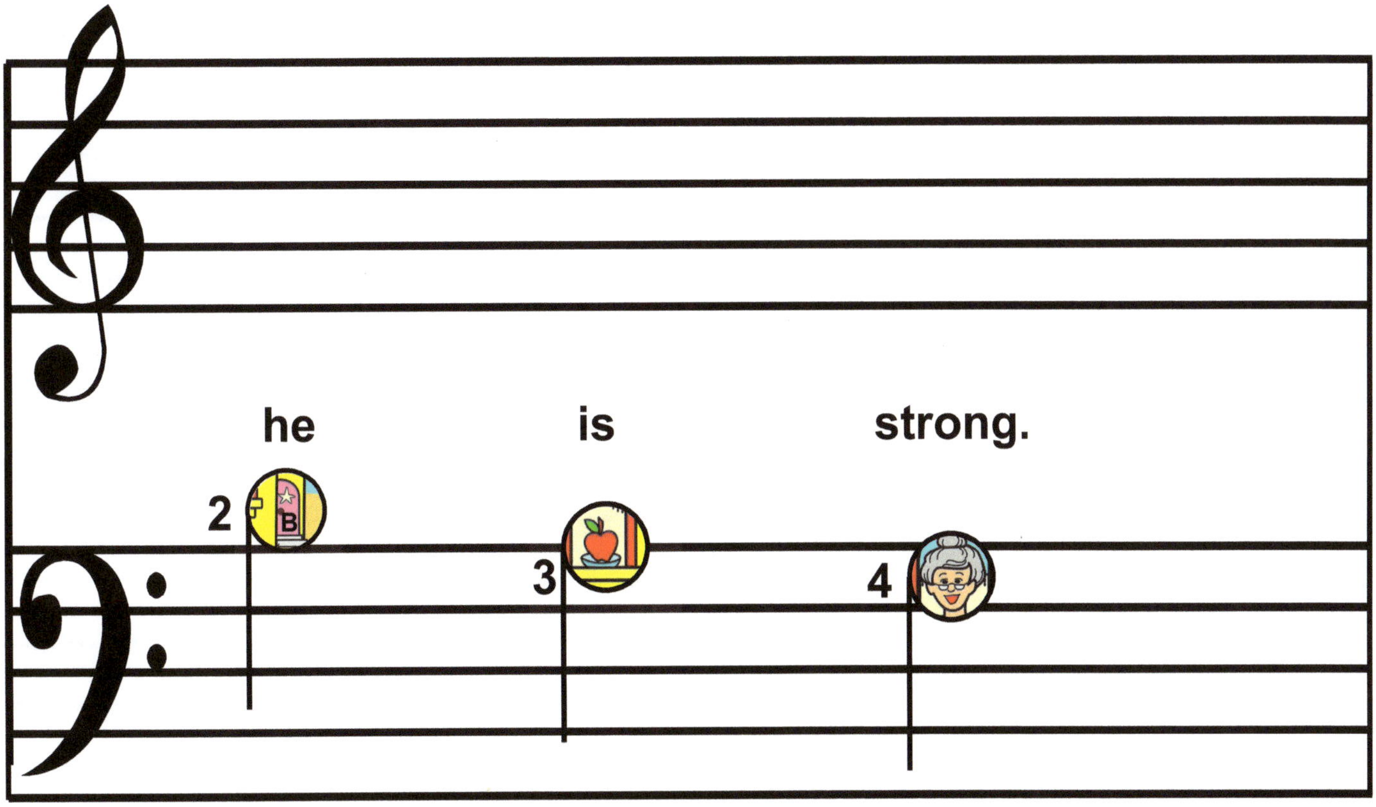 he is strong.

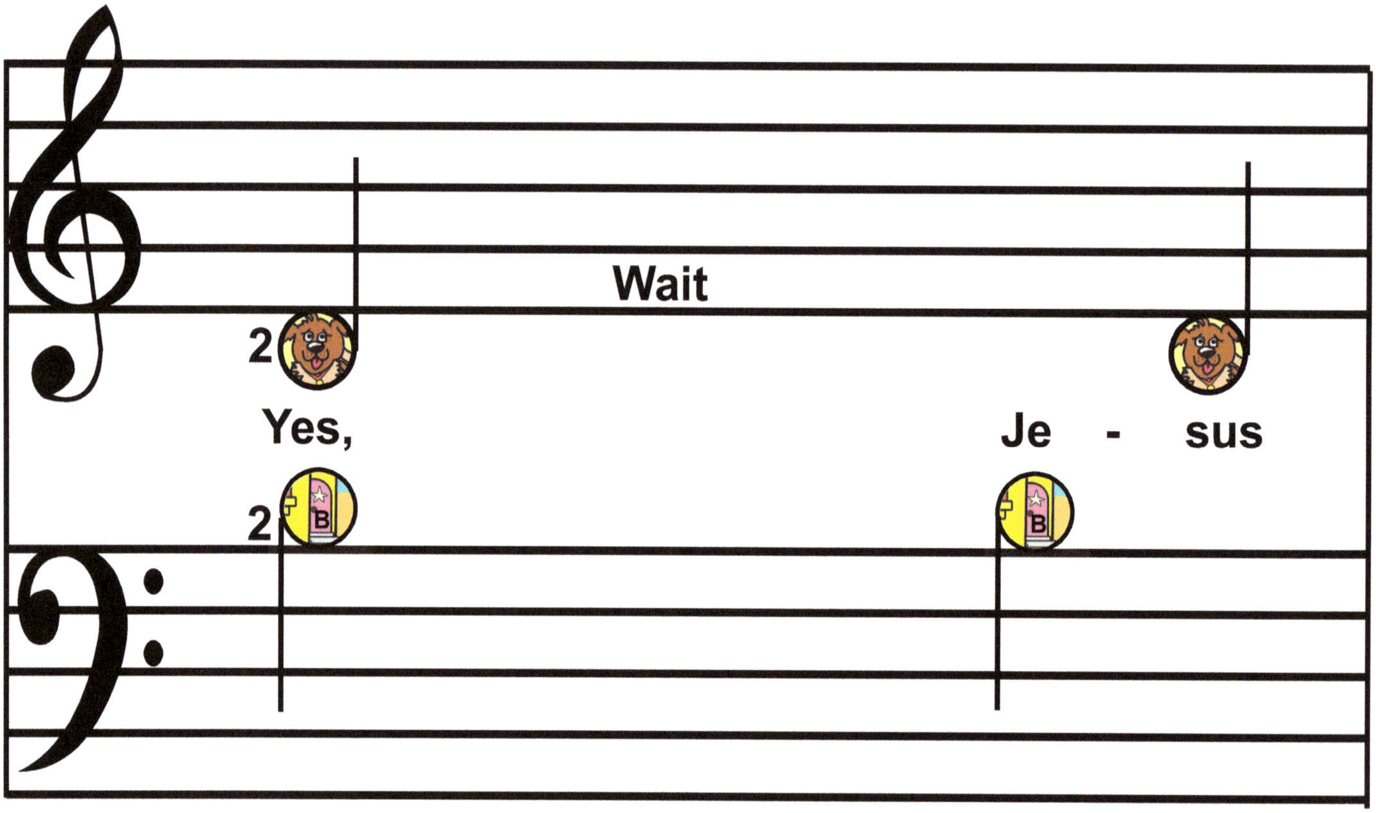

Wait

Yes, Je - sus

loves me,

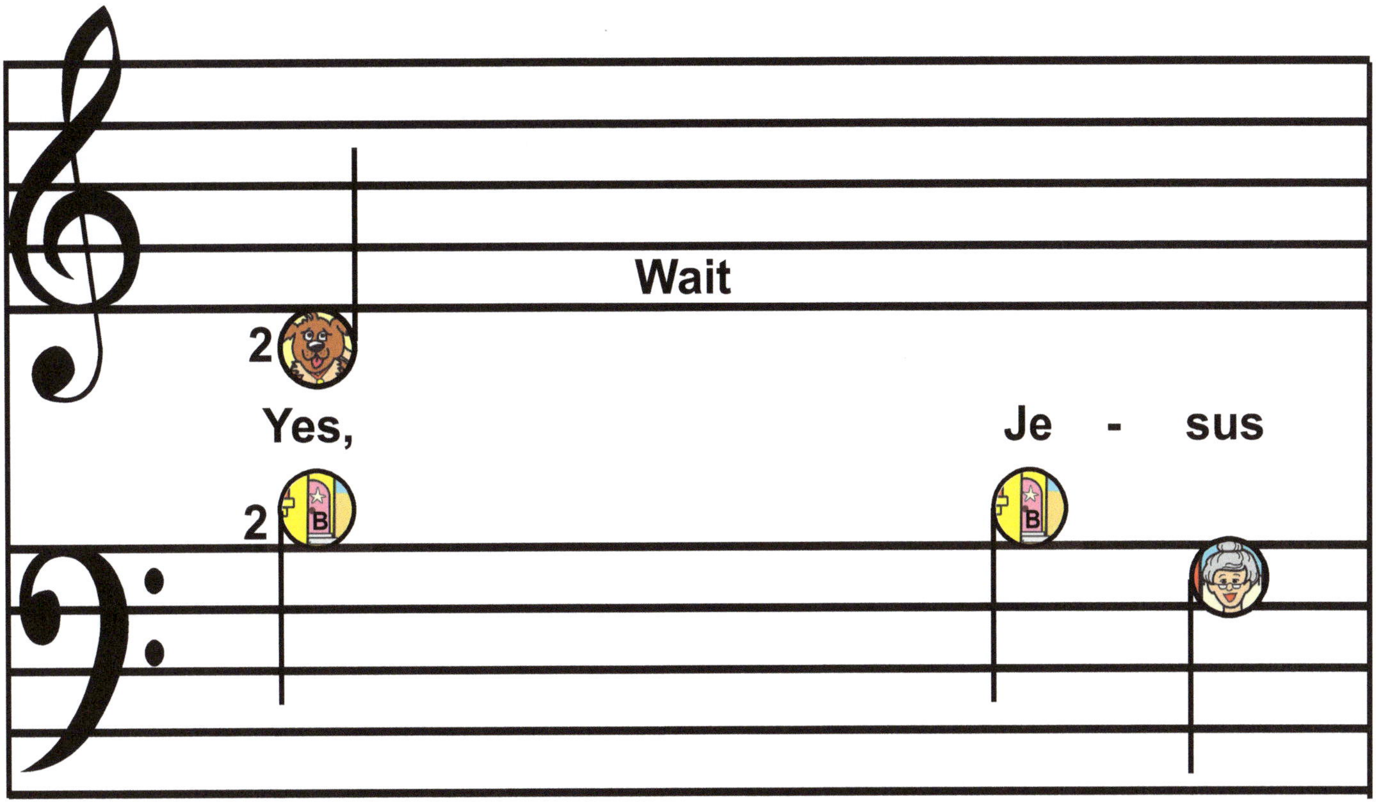

Wait

Yes, Je - sus

loves me,

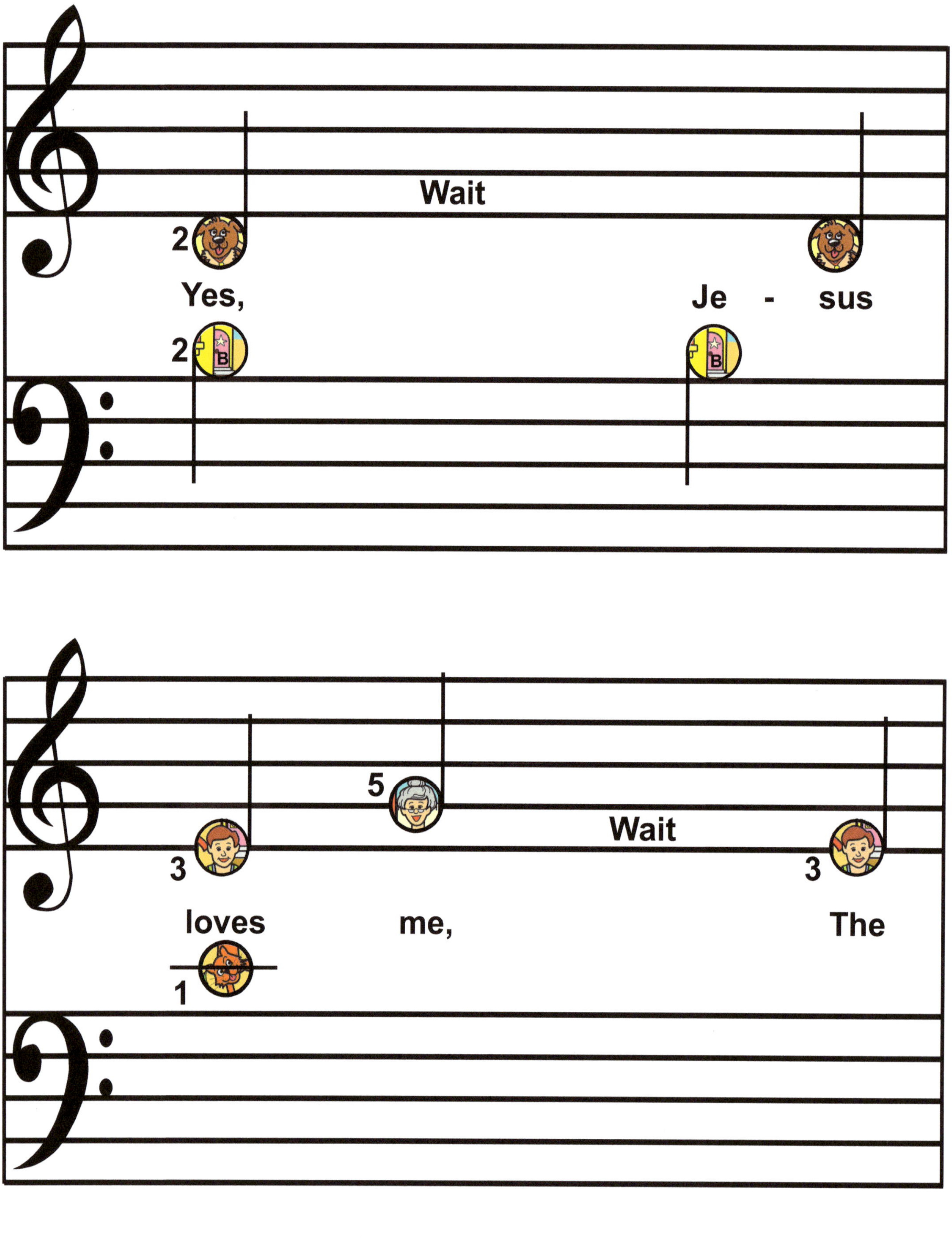

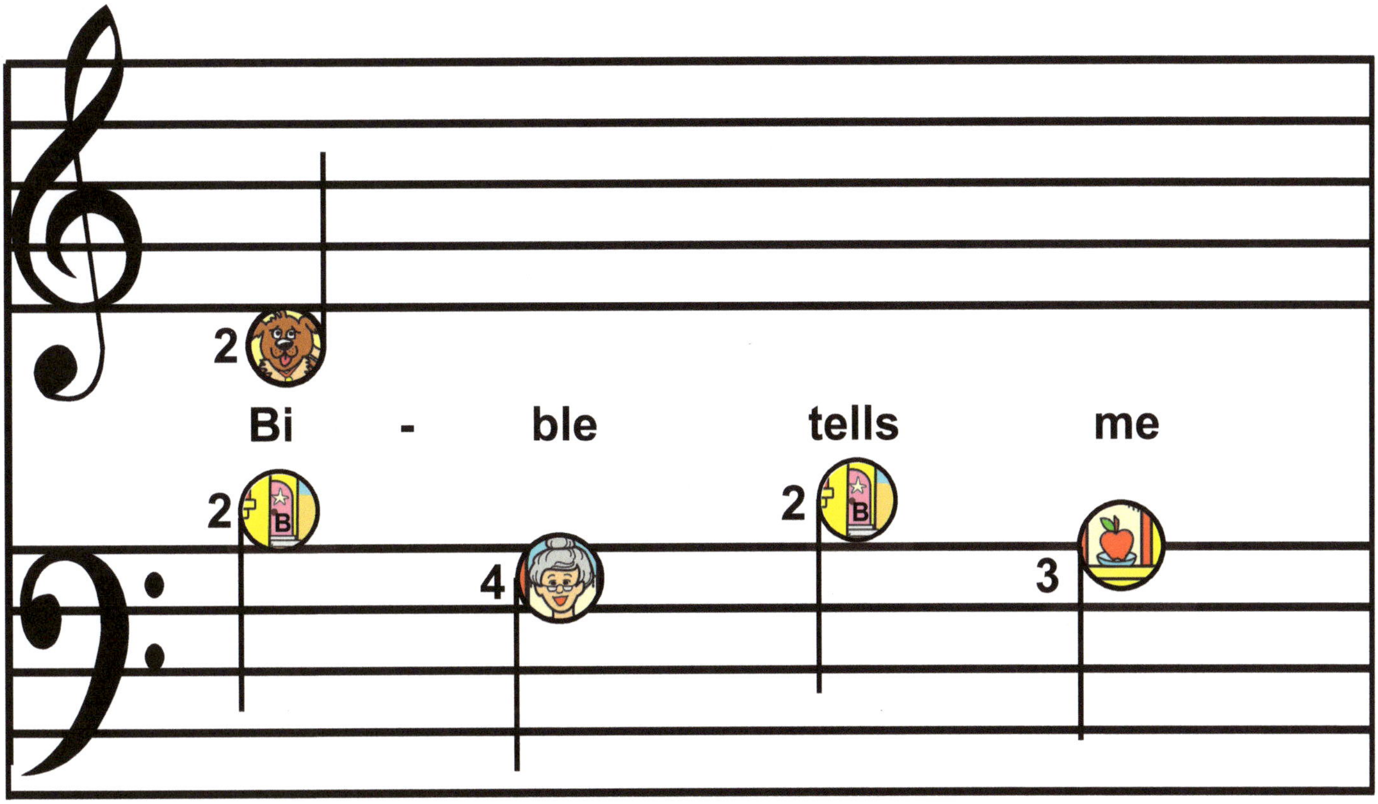

Bi - ble tells me

so.

About The Author

Karol Ann Krakauer lives in Colorado with her husband, Michael Patritch. She is a retired Certified Nurse-midwife who has continued to play piano and pipe organ since childhood. She has been teaching piano since high school to friends and family. Her goddaughter asked her to teach her four children piano. When the youngest child was 19 months old he decided it was time for him to have his lesson. He climbed onto the piano bench, pushed his brother off and looked to Karol Ann to give him his lesson. She started with the dog house, aka the two black notes, and made him the wooden doggie block to put in the dog house. Next she made him a grandma block with his grandma's photo on it to place in grandma's house, aka the three black notes and so on. The rest as they say is history.

photo by Nancy Langstaff Krakauer

Thanks to my husband, Michael, for the terrific help with editing. Thanks, also, to Ella whose wise nine year old editing was invaluable.

www.ingramcontent.com/pod-product-compliance
Lightning Source LLC
Chambersburg PA
CBHW042010150426
43195CB00002B/79